The Middle East: An Overview

THE LUCENT LIBRARY OF CONFLICT IN THE MIDDLE EAST

The Middle East:
An Overview

Other books in The Lucent Library of Conflict in the Middle East series include:

The Arab-Israeli Conflict
Human Rights in the Middle East
The Palestinians
U.S. Involvement in the Middle East: Inciting Conflict

THE LUCENT LIBRARY OF CONFLICT IN THE MIDDLE EAST

The Middle East: An Overview

By Diane Yancey

LUCENT BOOKS

An imprint of Thomson Gale, a part of The Thomson Corporation

THOMSON

★
TM

GALE

Detroit • New York • San Francisco • San Diego • New Haven, Conn. • Waterville, Maine • London • Munich

956.05
Yancey

LIBRARY OF CONGRESS CATALOGING-IN-PUBLICATION DATA

Yancey, Diane.
  The Middle East : an overview / by Diane Yancey.
    p. cm. — (Lucent library of conflict in the Middle East)
Includes bibliographical references.
  ISBN 1-59018-492-0
  1. Middle East—Juvenile literature. I. Title. II. Series.
DS44.Y365 2004
956.04—dc22

2004006205

Printed in the United States of America

CONTENTS

FOREWORD

On May 29, 2004, a group of Islamic terrorists attacked a housing compound in Khobar, Saudi Arabia, where hundreds of petroleum industry employees, many of them Westerners, lived. The terrorists ran through the complex, taking hostages and murdering people they considered infidels. At one point, they came across an Iraqi-American engineer who was Muslim. As the helpless stranger stood frozen before them, the terrorists debated whether or not he deserved to die. "He's an American, we should shoot him," said one of the terrorists. "We don't shoot Muslims," responded another. The militants calmly discussed the predicament for several minutes and finally came to an agreement. "We are not going to shoot you," they told the terrorized man. After preaching to him about the righteousness of Islam, they continued their bloody spree.

The engineer's life was spared because the terrorists decided that his identity as a Muslim overrode all other factors that marked him as their enemy. Among the unfortunate twenty-two others killed that day were Swedes, Americans, Indians, and Filipinos whose identity as foreigners or Westerners or, as the terrorists proclaimed, "Zionists and crusaders," determined their fate. Although the Muslim engineer whose life was spared had far more in common with his murdered coworkers than with the terrorists, in the militants' eyes he was on their side.

The terrorist attacks in Khobar typify the conflict in the Middle East today, where fighting is often done along factionalist lines. Indeed, historically the peoples of the Middle East have been unified not by national identity but by intense loyalty to a tribe, ethnic group, and above all, religious sect. For example, Iraq is home to Sunni Muslims, Shiite Muslims, Kurds, Turkomans, and Christian Assyrians who identify themselves by ethnic and religious affiliation first, and as Iraqis second. When conflict erupts, ancient, sometimes obscure alliances determine whom they fight with and whom they fight against. Navigating this complex labyrinth of loyalties is key to understanding conflict in the Middle East, because these identities generate not only passionate allegiance to one's own group but also fanatic intolerance and fierce hatred of others.

Russian author Anton Chekhov once astutely noted, "Love, friendship, respect do not unite people as much as a common hatred for something." His words serve as a slogan for conflict in the Middle East, where religious belief and tribal allegiances perpetuate strong codes of honor and revenge, and hate is used to motivate people to join in a common cause. The methods of generating hatred in the Middle East are pervasive and overt. After Friday noon prayers, for example, imams in both Sunni and Shiite mosques deliver fiery sermons that inflame tensions between the sects that run high in nearly every Muslim country where the two groups coexist. With similar intent to incite hatred, Iranian satellite television programs broadcast forceful messages to Shiite Muslims across the Middle East, condemning certain groups as threats to Shiite values.

Perhaps some of the most astounding examples of people bonding in hatred are found in the Israeli-Palestinian conflict. In the Palestinian territories, men, women, and children are consistently taught to hate Israel, and even to die in the fight for Palestine. In spring 2004, the terrorist group Hamas went so far as to launch an online children's magazine that demonizes Israel and encourages youths to become suicide bombers. On the other hand, some sectors of Israeli society work hard to stereotype and degrade Palestinians in order to harden Israelis against the Palestinian cause. Is-

raeli journalist Barry Chamish, for example, dehumanizes Palestinians when he writes, "The Palestinians know nothing of the creation of beauty, engage in no serious scholarship, pass nothing of greatness down the ages. Their legacy is purely of destruction."

This type of propaganda inflames tensions in the Middle East, leading to a cycle of violence that has thus far proven impossible to break. Terrorist organizations send suicide bombers into Israeli cities to retaliate for Israeli assassinations of Palestinian leaders. The Israeli military, in response, leads incursions into Palestinian villages to demolish blocks upon blocks of homes, shops, and schools, further impoverishing an already desperate community. To avenge the destruction and death left in the wake of the incursions, Palestinians recruit more suicide bombers to launch themselves at civilian targets in Israeli cities. Neither side is willing to let a violent attack go unreciprocated, undermining nonviolent attempts to mediate the conflict, and the vicious cycle continues.

The books in the Lucent Library of Conflict in the Middle East help readers understand this embattled region of the world. Annotated bibliographies provide readers with ideas for further research, while fully documented primary and secondary source quotations enhance the text. Each book in the series explores a different facet of conflict in the Middle East; together they provide students with a wealth of information as well as launching points for further study and discussion.

INTRODUCTION

Region in Turmoil

Mention the Middle East and many people think of deserts, camels, oil, or men kneeling in prayer. Some think of Cleopatra or the Bible, and remember that the region is the site of such ancient civilizations as Phoenicia, Babylon, and Egypt, as well as the birthplace of Judaism, Christianity, and Islam. Others, however, think of grim-faced Israeli soldiers or protesters shouting anti-American slogans. They point out that, today, the Middle East is a volatile and dangerous place because of ethnic, religious, and political tensions. "The Middle East is the most troubled region of a turbulent world. Its people are not at peace with one another, or with themselves, and they tend to feel that outsiders do not understand them,"[1] notes historian Arthur Goldschmidt Jr.

Diversity has something to do with the unrest. Over a quarter of a billion people with different customs, cultures, and objectives live crowded into this relatively small region. Muslims jostle against Jews, monarchies exist side by side with dictatorships, and Islamic fundamentalists walk the same streets as pro-Western businessmen.

There is even diversity when it comes to definition of the area. Some experts describe the Middle East as stretching from the Mediterranean Sea to Afghanistan. Some omit Afghanistan but include all North African nations. Some even draw Greece and Cyprus into the mix. To avoid confusion, this book defines the Middle East as the area around the eastern Mediterranean, which includes the countries of Turkey, Lebanon, Israel, Syria, Jordan, Iraq, Iran, Egypt, Tunisia, and Libya. It also includes the oil-producing nations of the Arabian Peninsula: Bahrain, Kuwait, Oman, Qatar,

Saudi Arabia, the United Arab Emirates, and Yemen.

Although all these nations are close to each other geographically, even the most similar are as different as the United States is from Great Britain or France. "The Middle East is a diverse and complex set of societies, and there can be no 'one size fits all' solution to the region's problems,"[2] noted Assistant Secretary of State for Near Eastern Affairs William Burns in March 2003.

A Multitude of Issues

There are a multitude of issues other than diversity that lead to conflict in the Middle East. Religious intolerance is a prime cause of violence. The controversial establishment of the Jewish state of Israel in the midst of millions of Muslims has led to invasions, wars, assassinations, and numerous ineffec-

tual peace efforts. In recent years, attacks against Israelis and their allies have caused widespread bloodshed and dimmed the chance of peace.

Autocratic governments are another cause of conflict. Tyrannical and dishonest leaders make many people in the Middle East feel angry and resentful. Yet most are unfamiliar with Western principles of democracy and tolerance that tend to promote peace and compromise. They have experienced change primarily as a result of coups, rebellions, or other violent events, and thus are prone to choose confrontation rather than dialogue when disagreements arise.

Interference from outside countries has also contributed to upheaval. In its position at the crossroads of Asia, Europe, and Africa, the Middle East has been invaded many times over the centuries. In 500 B.C. Alexander the Great

Common Background

Jews and Muslims often see each other as enemies, but in fact the two groups have much in common, including a rich past, a history of subjugation, and dreams of a homeland. Arthur Goldschmidt Jr. explains these commonalities further in his book A Concise History of the Middle East.

Jews and Arabs [an ethnic term for Middle Eastern Muslims] have some common traits. Both speak Semitic languages [a group that includes Arabic, Hebrew, and Aramaic] and they often look alike. Each looks back to a golden age early in its history, to an era of political power, economic prosperity, and cultural flowering. For each people, that era was followed by a long span of time during which their political destinies were controlled by outsiders. Due to their long subjugation, the birth of nationalism (which began in the late nineteenth century for both Jews and Arabs) was slow, painful, and uncertain. . . . Both suspected others of exploiting them. Both feared that, when the chips were down, the whole world would turn against them.

of Macedonia (Greece) defeated the Persians and claimed the Middle East as part of his empire. The legions of Rome took control of part of the region in the first century, and in the tenth century, Western crusaders arrived and carried out a series of holy wars against Muslims and Jews. In the thirteenth century, the Ottomans—Turkish Muslims—conquered the region, only to be defeated by the British and French, who became administrators of the remnants of the empire in 1914. During the twentieth century, the United States used its power and influence to manipulate the leadership, policies, and economics of countries there as well.

The region's vast oil fields have motivated most of the outside interference in modern times. Much of the world's oil wealth lies along the Persian Gulf, a finger of the Arabian Sea surrounded by Iran, Kuwait, Saudi Arabia, Oman, the United Arab Emirates, Bahrain, and Qatar. Efforts to control that wealth have led to much scheming by Western as well as Middle Eastern powers. In the words of Irving Kett, former director of operations of the U.S. Joint Chiefs of Staff, "The strategic importance of the vast petroleum [oil] reserves in the Middle East . . . requires the United States [and other Western nations] to consider this region carefully in formulating its foreign policy decisions."[3]

External and internal conflicts have all been made worse by an upsurge of terrorism in the region. A growing

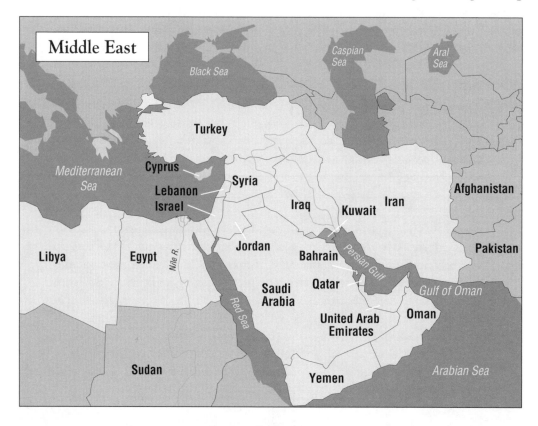

Middle East

Black Sea
Caspian Sea
Aral Sea
Turkey
Cyprus
Mediterranean Sea
Lebanon
Syria
Israel
Afghanistan
Iraq
Iran
Kuwait
Libya
Egypt
Nile R.
Jordan
Bahrain
Persian Gulf
Pakistan
Saudi Arabia
Qatar
Red Sea
Gulf of Oman
United Arab Emirates
Oman
Sudan
Yemen
Arabian Sea

Compelling Challenges

As Deborah J. Gerner notes in Understanding the Contemporary Middle East, *the people of the region face a multitude of challenges. She hopes, however, that the very diversity and determination that divides them will help them achieve peace and prosperity in the future.*

The twenty-first century opens with the Middle East oscillating between modernity and traditionalism, secularism and religious resurgence, economic growth and stagnation, peace and war. The tasks facing the peoples and governments of the region are compelling: it will not be easy to break free of the legacy of colonialism, address long-standing domestic and international conflicts, pursue economic and political development, and (re)create an identity (or identities) that can bring people together rather than split them into ever-more-narrowly defined groups. Fortunately, the people of the Middle East—Arabs, Persians, Israelis, Turks, and others—bring a diverse array of skills, aspirations, and resources that will aid them in this endeavor.

number of people in the Middle East are disillusioned with their lives and filled with hate and a desire for revenge against those they believe have repressed or exploited them. They use religion to validate their hate and violence as a quick and dramatic means of achieving their ends. World Bank president James Wolfensohn observes, "The face of [Osama] bin Laden, the terrorism of al-Qaeda, the rubble of the World Trade Center and of the Pentagon . . . are just symptoms. The disease is the discontent seething in Islam and, more generally, in the world of the poor."[4]

Everyone's Problem

In today's global society, conflicts in the Middle East cannot be easily brushed aside. They touch too many aspects of people's lives. For example, drivers in the United States pay high prices at the gas pump when anti-American sheikhs raise oil prices. Travelers submit to long security lines and incursions on their privacy because of threats from suicide bombers who hold Americans responsible for the problems of the Middle East. And young Americans in the military are called to intervene when brutal dictators threaten the region and the world.

The attacks on the United States on September 11, 2001, made clear that terrorists are a deadly expression of Middle Eastern resentment against the United States and the West. The attacks emphasized that all world citizens should be concerned about trying to bring peace to the region. First, however, the issues—numerous and complex—must be fully understood. There is too much at stake in the region known as "the cradle of Western civilization" for the discord to be ignored.

CHAPTER 1

Holy Ground: Religion in the Middle East

R eligion plays a key role in the Middle East, and much of the conflict that has marked the region for the past century and more is related to religious differences. Muslims are most numerous, but not all sects of Islam get along. Also present in the region are Jews, a variety of types of Christians, and other groups such as the Baha'is, the Druze, and the Zoroastrians, to name a few. For most of these people, religious beliefs are not simply commitments of worshipping at a mosque or synagogue once a week or observing special religious holidays. Instead, religion defines who they are, the way they act, the laws they follow, their loyalties, friends, and enemies.

Because religion touches so many aspects of life, certain groups disagree on how their society should be formed, and many are unwilling to compromise their desires because they believe they are approved by God. Two of the most antagonistic groups are Jews and Palestinian Muslims, whose hatred for each other sparks continued conflict in the region. News commentator John Loeffler explains:

> The two groups competing for the same space in the Middle East have two different religions, two different worldviews, two different "scriptures" for the future destiny of the land. Coupled with that is a century of bloodshed, conflict, reprisals and hatred in which populations of both sides have been caught, suffered and died.[5]

Rightful Owners?

The conflicts that exist between religious groups in the Middle East are more understandable when viewed in the light of history. According to the Jewish faith, God gave his people, the Hebrews—ancestors of today's Jews—the land of Canaan (called Palestine or Israel) sometime around 2100 B.C. when he established a relationship with Bible patriarch Abraham. Later, about 1450 B.C., the Bible claims that God directed Moses to lead the Hebrews out of slavery in Egypt and into that land, present-day Israel.

Jews pray at Jerusalem's Western Wall, one of Judaism's holiest sites.

They successfully established themselves there about 1400 B.C.

Because of God's pledge, Jews thus viewed themselves as the rightful owners of the holy land of Israel. In addition, they are tied to the land through innumerable historical places such as the tomb of patriarchs Abraham, Isaac, and Jacob in Hebron, and the fortress of Masada, the site of Jewish resistance against the Romans in the first century. Of particular significance is Jerusalem, King David's capital city. Within it stands the Holy Mount, site of the first Jewish temple built by King Solomon; the mount is also the historic site of Abraham's near-sacrifice of his son Isaac, an event recounted in the Old Testament of the Bible. Also located in Jerusalem is the Western Wall (or Wailing Wall), the remaining side of the second temple built by returning Jewish exiles about 536 B.C. Devout Jews traditionally go to the Western Wall to pray.

Although the majority of Jews became scattered throughout the world over time as a result of conquest and persecution, they yearned to return to their biblical homeland. Some even believed that going back to the region was a necessary condition to be met before their Messiah (savior) could come to earth. Because of this desire, Jews began returning to Palestine in large numbers in the early twentieth century. The formation of the modern nation of Israel in 1948 was a significant event for Jews throughout the world. In Israel, they felt like they were home.

"Indulgence in Delusion"

Islam is a source of direction and comfort to people in the Middle East, many of whom are poor and frustrated. As author Milton Viorst explains in the National Geographic Society's Cradle and Crucible: History and Faith in the Middle East, *the Koran, the holy book of Islam, promises that the afterlife will be much more meaningful than the good or bad times of the present.*

The Koran is an austere document, reflecting the desert culture from which it emerged. Meant as a sequel to the Bible, it contains some biblical references, but it is without the human dramas that are familiar to Bible readers. Similarly, it is short on history, providing few clues to the nature of the times. In our own age, many of its words and its references are obscure, even to scholars. Much of the Koran consists of divine admonitions directed at everyday life. If there is a theme, it is that life's real meaning lies not on Earth but in the eternal afterlife.

"Recognize," says the text . . . "that the life of this world is indulgence in delusion, idle talk, pageantry, boasting and rivalry over flaunted wealth and offspring. . . . But by and by, vegetation dries up, turns yellow before your eyes and becomes straw. That is how it is with the vanities of this life, which is all illusion. But in the hereafter, there is also grievous punishment, and God's forgiveness."

They could live as they pleased, worship freely, and teach their children to be proud of their heritage. Former prime minister Ehud Barak noted in 2000, "The revival of the State of Israel is . . . an act of supreme historic justice; there is nothing above it. Because of this, I swear that there will never again be a Jew without a home."[6]

Children of the Prophet

Muslims also saw the Middle East as the heart of their faith, Islam, and believed their claims on the land were just as strong as those of the Jews. Not only were they the majority in the region but places holy to Islam lay all around them. Mecca in Saudi Arabia was home of the prophet Muhammad and is the most sacred site among Muslims. The city of Medina is the second most holy site, and home to the Mosque of the Prophet, where Muhammad's tomb lay. Jerusalem contains the Al-Aqsa Mosque and the nearby Dome of the Rock, a golden domed structure that encloses the rock from which Muhammad was said to have ascended into heaven for a time. Al-Aqsa and the dome make up the third most sacred site of Islam.

The Islamic faith arose about the year A.D. 610 when a trader named Muhammad, a member of the Hashimite tribe in Saudi Arabia, claimed to have received a revelation from God directing him to become a divine messenger to the pagan people around him. Muhammad's message began with the pronouncement that there is only one all-powerful, all-knowing God who created the universe. Muhammad's teachings later expanded and were recorded in the Muslim holy book, the Koran. "There is no god but God, and Muhammad is his messenger,"[7] became the declaration of faith of Muslims everywhere.

A large community of Jews lived in Arabia, and Muhammad respected them and saw himself as another of their prophets. The Jews rejected him as a prophet, however, because many of his teachings contradicted or diverged from their scriptures. Believing his prophecy was correct, Muhammad founded the Muslim religion. Islam (which literally means "to submit") quickly became a unique philosophy, and thousands of devout converts began spreading its message of living a pure life and giving allegiance to Allah (God) throughout the world.

Islam expanded dramatically under Ottoman rule from the thirteenth through the twentieth century. By 1900, about 50 million Muslims lived in the Middle East. All leaders in the region were Muslim, about 90 percent of the population was Muslim, and anyone not of the Muslim faith was viewed as a second-class citizen. Jews and Christians—known as "People of the Book" because they, too, had sacred texts—were allowed to practice their own religion with little persecution, but they were required to live in their own neighborhoods and pay special taxes.

The Pilgrims

Christians were never the majority faith in the Middle East and did not view the region as given to them by God. Their reverence for the land stemmed from the fact that it was the setting for the Bible, as well as the place where Jesus Christ was born, lived, and died. Christian pilgrimages to the Holy Land began in the fourth century A.D. Most travelers made a point of visiting Bethlehem, Jesus' birthplace; Golgotha, the site of his death; the Church of the Holy Sepulcher, where he was buried; and the Mount of Olives, where he ascended to heaven.

As Islam gained converts in the seventh century, European Christians came to see Muslims as a threat to Christianity. Jerusalem and Bethlehem had come under Muslim rule in about A.D. 637. The Dome of the Rock had been constructed in 691 on the same site that Old Testament king Solomon's temple had stood. The temple had been revered by Christians as God's holy house. The presence of the Muslim dome seemed a slap in the face to them.

Many Christians felt that Muslims needed to be driven out of the Holy Land and the sacred sites reclaimed. The most powerful sponsor of this belief was Pope Urban II, who launched the first of a series of holy wars, known as the Crusades, in about 1095. Urban and other popes after him asked Christians all over western Europe to journey to Palestine and expel the Muslims.

Thousands took the challenge. The crusaders were successful in retaking parts of the Middle East, but their efforts to conquer or kill every Muslim in the region were fruitless. Land that was captured was soon lost again, and the Muslims retook Jerusalem in 1187. Christians remained a minority in the Middle East.

Sacred City

Because religion is a defining part of life for Jews, Muslims, and Christians in the Middle East, holy sites hold a great deal of significance. As the Crusades illustrated, when those sites are shared, conflict is the result.

The control of Jerusalem has always been a very contentious issue. Since World War II, conflicting claims to the city and its holy sites have regularly led to violence between Muslims and Jews. In 1947, when the United Nations recommended that Jerusalem be made an international city, war erupted over its control. Fought over again in the Six-Day War in 1967, the city was captured by the Israelis, who control it to the present. Jerusalem remains divided into Israeli and Palestinian neighborhoods, with most Palestinians concentrated in the eastern sectors, including what is known as the Old City.

The Holy Mount in Jerusalem is a flashpoint for trouble. In 1990, about twenty Muslims trying to worship at the Al-Aqsa Mosque were killed during fights with Jewish police. Another incident occurred in September 1996 when fifty-four Muslims and fourteen Jews were killed in a skirmish over an archaeological tunnel that Israel had opened under Al-Aqsa. Muslims feared that opening the tunnel would provide extremists an opportunity to destroy the mosque.

In September 2000, a visit to the mosque area by Israeli leader Ariel Sharon sparked violent demonstrations by outraged Muslims. Their protests developed into what became known as the "Al-Aqsa intifada"—a wave of violence that lasted

Crusading Christian soldiers invade Jerusalem, hoping to expel all Muslims from Palestine.

for years. And in July 2001, Palestinian Muslims began throwing stones down on Jewish worshippers at the Western Wall after a small group of extremists tried to place a cornerstone for a new Jewish temple on the Temple Mount. Although the extremists were not allowed near Al-Aqsa, Muslims described the event as an attempt to destroy Islamic shrines and lashed out against it.

Other Battle Sites

Jerusalem is not the only city where religious clashes have occurred. In May 1980, Palestinian activists attacked a group of Jews who were returning from prayers at the Tomb of the Patriarchs in the West Bank city of Hebron. Six Jews were killed and twenty were wounded. Hebron is the oldest Jewish community in the world, and is also the site of the grave of Sarah, Abraham's wife, and the locale where David was proclaimed king. The city was captured by the nation of Jordan in 1948 and became a Muslim community until the Israeli army recaptured it in June 1967. Jews began living there in 1979, angering the native Muslim populace.

In Bethlehem (also on the West Bank) in 1996, a Palestinian march past the Tomb of Rachel, a Jewish matriarch, turned violent as hundreds of Palestinian youths confronted Israeli troops guarding the site. The youths broke through a roadblock and hurled rocks at the troops, who fired tear gas and rubber-coated bullets in return.

In October 2000, an Israeli policeman died as a result of wounds sustained while trying to guard Joseph's Tomb in the West Bank town of Shechem. The tomb, which reportedly contains the bones of Jewish patriarch Joseph, had been attacked by Palestinians who threw firebombs and stones in an effort to destroy it.

Violence has occurred in other countries as well. In April 2002, a synagogue in Djerba, Tunisia, was destroyed in a bombing carried out by Muslim extremists. At least eighteen people were killed in the blast. And in November 2003, militant Muslims bombed several Jewish synagogues in Turkey. Twenty-four people were killed and over three hundred were wounded in these blasts.

Jew Versus Jew

Just as tension exists between Muslims and Jews, discord occurs between Jewish Israelis who hold differing views about religion and its place in their society. Most disputes arise between members of ultra-Orthodox (conservative) religious groups and secular groups. The former believe the nation should revolve around God and the Torah (Jewish law), while the latter want the country to emphasize Jewish ethnicity, not religion.

Although a large portion of the Israeli population is nonobservant (that is, not religious), religious political parties exercise a strong influence on the Israeli government. No leader can get elected without their support, and they are able to dictate many aspects of political policy. For instance, they determine who can and cannot become an Israeli citizen, that Orthodox Judaism will be the state religion, and whether Orthodox Jews get privileges, such as free private schooling. "Many ordinary Israelis are increasingly fed up at seeing their taxes going to fund religious seminaries whose students avoid military service,"[8] observes BBC reporter Jonathan Marcus, referring to a policy that allows ultra-Orthodox religious students to get military draft deferments. The majority of eighteen-year-old Israelis are required to serve in the military.

Disputes between Jews rarely become physical, but violence has occurred at times. For instance, in the mid-1980s bombs were placed in newsstands in the Orthodox Bnei Brak suburb of Tel Aviv where nonreligious newspapers were being sold. The explosives effectively warned the owners that secular views would not be tolerated in the conservative neighborhood.

Ultra-Orthodox Jews have repeatedly scuffled with liberal Jews who try to pray at the Western Wall as well. In 1999 police had to intervene when a group of American non-Orthodox rabbis—some of them women—approached the wall. Orthodox believers oppose the equal participation of women during worship.

In the 1990s, ultra-Orthodox Jews clashed with police over their demands that a main street of Jerusalem be closed to traffic on a weekly religious holiday known as the Sabbath. Jewish ritual law forbids the operation of machinery, including cars, on their day of worship, which lasts from Friday night to Saturday night.

Muslim Versus Muslim

Just like Jews, Muslims disagree among themselves, and their disagreements—especially if they revolve around holy sites—sometimes lead to violence. For instance, Muslim government forces fought against Muslim extremists in Saudi Arabia in 1979 after the extremists seized the Grand Mosque of Mecca. The extremists were protesting the royal family's relationship with Western governments and businesses, whom they saw as liberal. In the fighting over the mosque, which lasted two weeks, 250 people were killed.

Differences between two major Muslim sects—Sunnis and Shiites—account for much of the conflict between Muslims. Sunni Muslims make up the largest branch of Islam. They believe that leadership should be in the hands of the Muslim community, and accept the authority

Fundamental Issue

Differences between Jewish groups in Israel were addressed in 1998 by journalist Jonathan Marcus in an Internet article titled "Secularism vs. Orthodox Judaism," found on the BBC News Web site.

Quite apart from differences over the peace process or economic policy, one fundamental fault line is threatening to split Israeli society into two: that between the ultra-orthodox Jewish religious constituency on the one hand and the secular [nonreligious] majority on the other. . . .

The Jewishness of Israel is a complex issue. . . . In large part the problem is an outgrowth of Israel's highly—some might say—over-representative political system. Here, ultra-orthodox political parties, many of whom do not accept the existence of the Jewish state, are able to wield significant political influence. . . . These . . . unworldly people would argue that the creation of Israel is premature and should await the coming of a messianic age [when the savior returns and brings peace] . . . [still] they are quite happy to secure as large a share of state subsidies [money] as they can for their religious institutions. . . .

Many ordinary Israelis are increasingly fed up at seeing their taxes going to fund religious seminaries whose students avoid military service. They do not want to fund a parallel school system that prevents religious and secular children from mixing. There are worrying danger signals; physical attacks for example on some ultra-orthodox Jews. It is this issue more than any other that will determine what sort of society Israel is to become. And it is one with which the mainstream politicians will ultimately have to grapple.

of the first four caliphs (seventh-century Islamic leaders). They believe these men were the rightful successors to Muhammad. Shiite Muslims, however, believe that leadership should have stemmed from a line of descent starting with Muhammad's cousin and son-in-law, Ali. They believe that Muhammad selected his first twelve successors by name and that these men inherited a special knowledge of the true meaning of the scripture that was passed from father to son, beginning with the Prophet himself.

Differences between Sunnis and Shiites have sometimes been played out on the battlefield. Religious differences were part of the conflict that made up the Iran-Iraq War, a lengthy war that cost countless lives and millions of dollars. Iraq at that time was ruled by Sunnis, while Iran was mostly Shiite. Iran's Shiite leaders,

Thousands of Shiite Muslims gather for a religious ceremony in Iraq. Differences between Shiite and Sunni Muslims have led to conflict in the region.

Christian Minority

Faced with religious discrimination and violence, many Christians have fled the Middle East. Those that remain come from a variety of backgrounds, as author Charles M. Sennott explains in Cradle and Crucible: History and Faith in the Middle East, *edited by the National Geographic Society.*

As it has been from the very beginning of the faith, Christianity in the Middle East is diverse, encompassing Palestinians, Egyptians, Jordanians, Iraqis, and Syrians. Historically, the largest number of Christians have been followers of the Eastern Orthodox churches. . . . The second largest group in the Holy Land—roughly one third—are members of the Roman Catholic Church (or as it's often called in this part of the world, the Latin Church). The so-called Uniate churches—the Maronites, concentrated in Lebanon, and the Melkites, concentrated in Galilee— also acknowledge the primacy of Rome. . . . In addition to these denominations are small numbers of indigenous Lutherans, Anglicans, and Baptists.

All these manifestations of Christianity make for an ornate tapestry. But sadly, deep divisions, especially the bitter, thousand-year-old schism between Orthodoxy and Catholicism, too often have torn at this fabric of Christianity, contributing even further to its diminution. . . . Today, Christians of the Holy Land are an almost invisible minority, alienated from their own clerical hierarchy and ruled by foreign governments.

angry with Iraq's government, urged Iraq's Shiite population to rise up and overthrow Saddam Hussein's Sunni government. Iraqi Sunnis battled Iranian Shiites for eight long years until a cease-fire was called in 1988.

Sunnis and Shiites fought again in Iraq in 1991 when Shiites rebelled against Sunni Muslims in the city of Karbala, holy because of its shrine to Muhammad's grandson, Imam Hussein. Iraqi Shiites had for years been oppressed and ignored by the Sunnis, who had come to power with Saddam Hussein. After the Persian Gulf War of 1990–1991, they felt emboldened to push for greater religious expression.

By 2004, Sunni-Shiite conflicts were again on the rise as each group feared the other might gain control of Iraq's new government. On March 2, Shiites were attacked during one of their most sacred and solemn holidays, Ashura. More than 140 people were killed, some of them in midprayer. The attacks reminded the world of the rift between the two sects, and also of how difficult nation building in the Middle East could be.

Muslim Versus Christian

In modern times, few clashes have occurred between Muslims and Christians in the Middle East. One of the few, however, led to a civil war that lasted almost fifteen years. Lebanon, a country where Christians constitute a significant percentage of the population, gained its independence from France in 1943. Because the population was divided almost equally between the two faiths at that time, the government was set up so that Christians and Muslims shared power.

That division worked until the 1970s. By then, a higher birthrate among Muslims, coupled with influxes of Palestinian refugees from Israel and elsewhere, had shifted the population ratio in favor of Muslims. Christian leaders refused to make policy changes that would better represent the Muslim majority, however. That and other tensions propelled the nation into war in 1975. Between 1975 and 1990, almost 150,000 people were killed in fighting between Muslim and Christian militia groups. The country suffered an estimated $25–$30 billion in damage and lost revenues. Beirut—once a cosmopolitan city—was virtually destroyed.

Even today, tensions linger between the country's Christians and Muslims. "The war in Lebanon left a lot of scars and it's not easy for Christians and Muslims to get together," says Habib Badr, pastor of the National Evangelical Church of Beirut. "In my view [the rebuilding is] still in its initial stage."[9]

With religious feelings so passionate in the region, it is unlikely that conflicts between various faiths and sects will fade in the near future. As has been demonstrated from Lebanon to Iraq, building better relationships among adherents of the various faiths and sects is not likely to be a quick or an easy task. In fact, for a region that boasts close connections to the same just and loving God, many who live there are anything but just and loving to one another.

CHAPTER 2

Outside Forces

C onflict in the Middle East, triggered by religious and other differences, has often been complicated and aggravated by outsiders. Usually the intruders believed their presence was justified to stop aggression, overthrow a dictator, keep the peace, or the like. Over time, however, occupation caused upheaval, tension, and resentment. Western occupiers in particular, with their European customs and points of view, had the most significant impact on the status quo, as historian Bernard Lewis observes: "Western political domination, economic penetration, and . . . cultural influence . . . changed the face of the region and transformed the lives of its people, turning them in new directions, arousing new hopes and fears, creating new dangers and new expectations."[10]

A Taste of the Outside World

Crusaders who settled in the region beginning in the tenth century gave people in the Middle East their first glimpse of Western culture—European languages, clothing, weaponry, and foods. Trade between Europe and the Middle East in the centuries that followed expanded that exposure.

Oil exploration led the British to the Middle East in about 1900, and the defeat of the Ottoman Empire by the Allies (Great Britain, France, Russia, the United States, and others) after World War I (1914–1918) left the region under the control of Western powers. Britain was made trustee (that is, put in charge) of the land that is now Iraq, Israel, and Jordan. France assumed trusteeship of Lebanon and Syria. The Allies attempted to parcel out parts of present-day Turkey, but Turkish soldier Mustafa

Western Wear

Change as a result of Western influence was first apparent in the armies of the Middle East. In his book The Middle East: A Brief History of the Last 2,000 Years, *historian Bernard Lewis explains how the adoption of both Western weaponry and Western uniforms was significant.*

Change in dress began, as did most aspects of modernization, with the military. For the reformers, Western military uniforms had a certain magic. As Muslim armies were defeated again and again on the battlefield by their infidel enemies, Muslim rulers reluctantly adopted not only the weaponry but also the organization and equipment of their opponents, including Western-style uniforms. When the first Ottoman reform troops were organized at the end of the eighteenth century, it was necessary for them to adopt Western drill and weapons; it was not necessary for them to adopt Western uniforms. This was a social, not a military choice, and it has been followed in virtually all modern armies in Muslim lands, including even Libya and the Islamic Republic of Iran. They have to use Western weapons and tactics because these are the most effective; they do not have to wear fitted tunics and peaked caps, but they still do. This change of style remains as a continuing testimony to the authority and attraction of Western culture, even among those who explicitly and vehemently reject it.

Kemal rallied national support and expelled outside forces from the country. The Turkish republic with Kemal as president was proclaimed in 1923.

The Middle Eastern peoples in countries managed by the British and French (who also lived among them) became second-class citizens in their own land. Considered crude and primitive by their European rulers, most lived in poverty, were poorly educated, and had no say over how their country was run. Western leaders were intolerant of rebellion, so the many revolts that were attempted were usually put down with force.

Voluntarily or involuntarily, however, people in the Middle East were exposed to Western ways and Western thinking during this time of European domination.

Some of the new concepts seemed strange and hard to grasp. For instance, the notion of national governments, parliaments, constitutions, political parties, and cabinets were not at first understood or appreciated. In addition, European clothing appeared impractical for hot desert climates, and European languages were awkward to speak.

Nevertheless, the new ways gradually became less jarring. The people also became familiar with Western religions, and learned of democracy and human rights from those children who were educated by European teachers. After centuries of authoritarian leadership under the Ottomans, these concepts were enlightening. Arthur Goldschmidt points out, "They learned that bad governments did not have to be endured, that individuals had rights and freedoms that should be protected."[11] Schools also encouraged students to adapt to changing times rather than cling to old, outmoded ways of thinking.

Conflicting Promises
In addition to their disruptive physical presence during this period, the British and French made conflicting promises to the people of the region, which had

Arabs leaving Jerusalem in 1938. Western domination of the Middle East during the early twentieth century exposed Arab residents to Western traditions and ideology.

long-term negative consequences. To gain support in their fight against the Ottomans during World War I, they promised a number of different Middle Eastern leaders that their people would be granted independence in return for collaboration. In a document known as the Balfour Declaration of November 1917, for example, the British promised to support the establishment of a national home in Palestine for Jews in order to win worldwide Jewish support for the war effort.

Unfortunately, the British had made a similar pact with the Arabs (Arabic-speaking people in the Middle East). The MacMahon-Hussein letters of 1915 promised that the British would support Arab aims of independence in Palestine if they agreed to fight with the British against the Ottomans. To complicate matters, the British and French drafted the secret Sykes-Picot Agreement of 1916. This agreement stipulated that the defeated Ottoman Empire would be divided between Britain, France, Italy, and Russia and be administered by them after the war.

Once they were made public, the conflicting commitments strained relationships among all parties involved. The pacts were obviously contradictory, seemed a betrayal of the agreements, and affronted the Middle Eastern leaders who had approved them. They also inspired further resentment among those who so passionately wanted independence. "Even if Britain and France governed their mandates well, promoting education and economic development, the Arabs wanted to rule themselves,"[12] explains Goldschmidt.

"Imposed from Above"

Westerners often acted arbitrarily when it came to drawing boundaries in the Middle East. They then expected the nations they created to be cohesive units. In his book From Beirut to Jerusalem, *author Thomas Friedman points out that their expectations were unreasonable.*

Many of the states in the Middle East today . . . were not willed into existence by their own people or developed organically out of a common historical memory or ethnic or linguistic [language] bond; they also did not emerge out of a social contract between rulers and ruled. Rather, their shapes and structures were imposed from above by the imperial powers. These shapes had little or no precedent in either the medieval or the ancient world. Rather, boundaries were drawn almost entirely on the basis of the foreign policy, communications, and oil needs of the Western colonial powers that were to dominate these new countries. . . . As a result, these states were like lifeboats into which various ethnic and religious communities, each with their own memories and their own rules of the game, were thrown together and told to row in unison, told to become a nation, told to root for the same soccer team and salute the same flag. Instead of the state growing out of the nation, the nation was expected to grow out of the state.

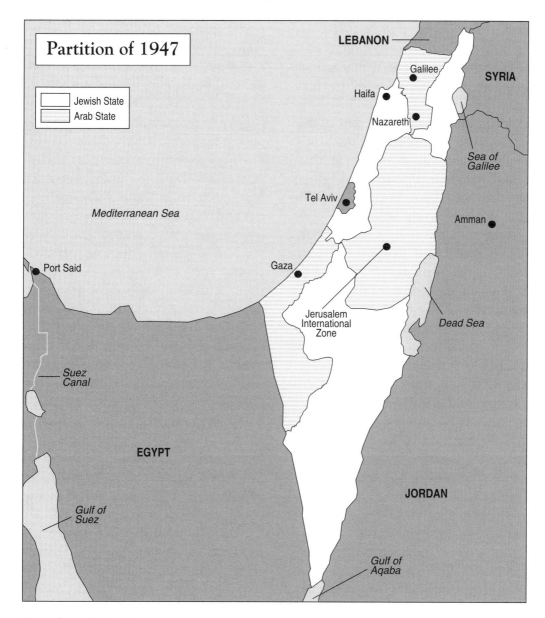

Partition of 1947

Jewish State
Arab State

LEBANON

Galilee

SYRIA

Haifa

Nazareth

Sea of
Galilee

Mediterranean Sea

Tel Aviv

Amman

Port Said

Gaza

Jerusalem
International
Zone

Dead Sea

Suez
Canal

EGYPT

JORDAN

Gulf of
Suez

Gulf of
Aqaba

Random Divisions

Perhaps the most ill considered decision made by Western powers involved the drawing of boundaries. The borders drawn to carve out the nation of Israel in particular ignored the rights and feelings of Arabs who lived in the region. They set the scene for conflict that continues to the present day.

In addition to discounting Arab feelings, Israel's borders were impractical from the beginning. They were originally laid down by the United Nations in 1947. The organization decided that the new nation would be three separate regions, connected only by narrow strips of land to allow passage between each section. Boundaries were based totally on demographics—that is, they encircled land where large populations of Jews already lived. Jerusalem was designated an international zone, thus leaving more than 100,000 Jews who resided in Jerusalem isolated from their country and surrounded by hostile Arabs. Eventually, through war, Israel seized enough land to make a contiguous state, but these conquests only further antagonized its neighbors.

When it came to dividing up the rest of the Middle East, Britain and France took it upon themselves to carve up the large region that had once been the Ottoman Empire. They again laid down borders according to their vision of what the region should look like. Their divisions had little or nothing to do with natural divisions between tribes, or ethnic and religious groups. For instance, Christians and Muslims, who shared few common desires and quarreled regularly, were required to govern together in Lebanon. In Iraq, Shiite Muslims, Sunni Muslims, and Muslim Kurds (a distinct ethnic and cultural group who inhabit the region as well) were grouped together despite strong religious, societal, and historical differences. Historian William Cleveland notes, "They [the three provinces of Iraq] were among the most ethnically and religiously diverse Arab regions of the Ottoman Empire, and their amalgamation [union] into a single country posed exceptionally difficult obstacles to nation building."[13]

Dependence on Outsiders

Outside interference continued in the Middle East throughout the twentieth century. Countries under trusteeships were granted independence, but most remained bound to their European administrators by treaties. Also, foreign military forces remained in the region. National governments tended to be unpopular and shaky, and relied on strong outside support to survive. This occurred for two reasons. First, the new leaders were relatively inexperienced, as Sandra Mackay observes: "Each of these territories had been left by the Ottomans with little in the way of governmental experience, physical infrastructure, public education, or social services. As a result, they lacked the most basic resources needed to begin the critical process of nation building."[14] The leaders also lacked legitimacy, since many had been chosen by European administrators instead of by the people. King Faisal bin Hussein, for instance, was a native of Saudi Arabia whom the British installed as ruler of Iraq in gratitude for his assistance during World War I. Despite good intentions, Faisal remained an outsider and never successfully established a sense of unity in Iraq's diverse society.

National governments also remained weak because nationalism—the desire to create, maintain, and have loyalty to a common country—was a foreign concept to most people in the Middle East. Many who lived in rural communities did not think in terms of nations. Villagers usually interacted with and obeyed a local tribal head who lived nearby. They also turned to him, or to other members of the family or tribe, for help and support. According to journalist Thomas Friedman, "Political identities tended to be drawn . . . either from one's religious affiliation or one's local kin group—be it the tribe, clan, village, neighborhood, sect, region, or professional association."[15]

Despite obstacles, however, nationalistic feelings slowly grew. People began to realize that national governments could benefit them in many ways. Programs that promoted education, health care, low-cost housing, rural electrification projects, and paved highways were especially conducive to increasing popular support for nationalism.

Caught in the Middle

As the twentieth century moved past its midpoint, the Cold War (political tension and military rivalry that stopped short of full-scale war) between the United States and the Communist-led Soviet Union added new complications in the Middle East. The Soviet Union, with an avowed goal of worldwide domination, recognized that its enemy, the United States, had vast influence in the region and around the world. To try to counterbalance that influence, the Soviets stepped in to the Middle East, providing arms and aid to countries such as Syria and Egypt in attempts to win them as allies.

The United States found a strong ally in Israel, another democracy, and also backed certain Muslim leaders who it believed would further American interests. These included the rulers of Iran and Saudi Arabia. Iraqi dictator Saddam Hussein was even at one point a U.S. ally, during the Iran-Iraq War of 1980–1988. At that time, Iran's new leader, the Ayatollah Khomeini, seemed the greater threat to American interests.

The two superpowers' involvement in the region had a variety of negative

Nationalism

In his book A Concise History of the Middle East, *Arthur Goldschmidt Jr. defines nationalism as "the desire of a large group of people to create or maintain a common statehood." He goes on to explain that the concept was unfamiliar to people in the Middle East but that, despite their traditions, it took root and flourished.*

Nationalism was itself foreign to the world of Islam. In traditional Islamic thought, the *ummah,* or community of believers, was the sole object of political loyalty for Muslims. Loyalty meant defending the land of Islam against rulers or peoples of other faiths. All true Muslims were supposed to be brothers and sisters, regardless of race, language, and culture. Although distinctions existed between Arabs and Persians, or between them and the Turks, common adherence to Islam was supposed to transcend all divergences. Nationalism should not exist in Islam.

Yet it does. . . . As Middle Easterners learned how to work like Europeans, they also leaned how to think like them. . . . While they faced the frustrations of these years [under Western control] and those that followed, their ideas crystallized into nationalist movements.

repercussions. First, it helped polarize the Middle East. It also gave opposing nations like Iran and Iraq the confidence to wage war, knowing that they had the backing of an influential ally. This created more instability and enormous devastation. For instance, weapons provided by the United States and the Soviets for the Iran-Iraq War ultimately killed at least 300,000 people and injured almost 1 million.

Safeguarding Western Interests

The United States was involved with the Middle East for economic as well as political reasons during the twentieth century. With a booming automobile industry, it needed friends in oil-rich countries to ensure that gasoline would be available at reasonable prices to American consumers.

Few U.S. leaders were bothered by the fact that many of the regimes they supported repressed their own people. Few cared that money from oil was going into the pockets of the rich, leaving the majority of the population very poor. And even the most compassionate and conciliatory U.S. leaders, like President Jimmy Carter, made it clear that the United States would go to great lengths to prevent anti-Western powers, such as the Soviet Union, from interfering with its relationships in the Middle East. Carter stated in 1980, "An attempt by any outside force to gain control of the Persian Gulf region will be regarded as an assault on the vital interests of the United States of America, and such an assault will be repelled by any means necessary, including military force."[16]

Such threats were not empty. When in 1990 Saddam Hussein invaded the small, oil-producing nation of Kuwait, President George H.W. Bush went to war, backed by a coalition of over thirty nations that opposed the aggression and feared that an Iraq-controlled Kuwait posed a threat to stable oil prices. They worried that Saddam would be able to cut oil production, drive up prices, or even use a further threat of force to pressure other oil nations into following his lead.

The involvement of Western nations in liberating Kuwait was supported worldwide, but the decision to station troops in Saudi Arabia during and after the war had unexpected ramifications. It was one of the primary reasons that Osama bin Laden declared war against the United States in 1998, marking the beginning of a new era of terrorism for the country.

Unwinnable Wars?

The United States was also trying to protect its interests when it launched the war against Saddam Hussein in early 2003. In addition to being a potential threat to Western oil supplies, Saddam was accused of developing nuclear and biological weapons that could be used against his enemies worldwide. In late 2002, after the dictator refused to comply with UN weapons inspectors, President George W. Bush sent one hundred thousand U.S. troops to Iraq to oust him and his repressive regime. The Iraq War began in March of the following year. "There is a conviction that the Iraqi regime constitutes a danger to the region and to its own peo-

U.S. troops battle Iraqi resistence fighters in 2003. Ousting Saddam Hussein from power was relatively easy, but rebuilding Iraq proved more difficult than expected.

ple and that the possession of weapons of mass destruction constitutes a danger beyond the region in the hands of that leadership,"[17] stated Richard Murphy, a former U.S. assistant secretary of state for Middle Eastern affairs.

Deposing Saddam was a relatively quick and painless operation. As U.S. troops entered Baghdad in April 2003, he fled the city, only to be captured eight months later. Reestablishing order in Iraq, including fighting insurgents, terrorist groups, and hostile civilians, however, promised to take longer. The United States had not taken into account the resentment Iraqis felt toward Westerners, or the long-term hostilities that existed between the different religious and ethnic groups in the country. "We are in a sand trap," conservative columnist Pat Buchanan stated in September 2003,

and the question the president and Congress must answer is: Do we go in deeper? Do we pour in whatever money and blood are needed to fight on to victory in a land where we are not loved and where the enemy can fight the kind of war Islamic warriors have fought successfully against the French in Algeria, the Russians in Afghanistan and the Israelis in Lebanon? Or do we disengage, [and] accept the humiliation of an American withdrawal?[18]

Buchanan's questions had been asked before, just as America had gotten involved in an unwinnable war in the Middle East before. When President Ronald Reagan sent U.S. troops into Lebanon in the 1980s in response to an attack on the American embassy in Beirut, the soldiers found themselves caught up in hostilities that were as bewildering as they were unsolvable. Political factions attacked each other. Christians fought against Muslims. Israeli and Syrian jets dueled in the skies. Marine sergeant Jeffrey Roberts said, "To me it was a civil war, only it wasn't just the North against the South. It was the North against South, East against West, Northeast against Southwest, Southeast against Northwest, and we were in the middle of it all. There were just too many different sides. If we picked one, we had four others against us."[19]

America learned a hard lesson in Lebanon. Getting involved in Middle Eastern problems might be tempting, but Western interference—even when sincere—seldom simplified matters. The presence of outsiders usually stirred already troubled waters. As a consequence, people in the Middle East were often left with more rather than fewer problems. As Sandra Mackay observed, "Arabs from the Nile to the Tigris, from the mountains of northern Iraq to the tip of Yemen, have struggled to find independence, identity, political stability, and social justice. Yet what they have experienced is foreign occupation, conflicted concepts of identity, [and] splintered societies."[20]

CHAPTER 3

Yours or Mine?

Arbitrary boundaries set by Western powers after World War I contributed to conflicts relating to religion, ethnicity, national identity, and international alliances in the Middle East. They also set the stage for clashes over borders, territory, scarce resources such as water, and profitable ones such as oil.

Indeed, oil and water have proven very important for countries set in a desert environment and endowed with few resources or industries that bring in income. Those nations that have access to water, ports, and agricultural land are able to successfully farm and trade. Those with oil have a fortune beneath their feet. Those that are not so lucky remain poor—or scheme and fight to get their share of the region's resources. This fighting over resources is not unique to the Middle East. Historian James J. Pu-

plava explains: "Throughout human history, natural resources have been the cause behind most wars. Nations wanted them and took them or tried to take them by going to war. . . . The side that prevails in war will be the side that can maintain a robust economy and control over resources vital to its economy."[21]

Black Gold

Oil, a vital resource because of the money it brings in, has been a major motivator of conflict in the Middle East. Oil reserves were discovered by the British in Iran about 1908, and were also identified in Iraq, Bahrain, Kuwait, Qatar, and Saudi Arabia. Shortly thereafter, oil began to play a major role in the world economy.

The growth of the petroleum industry marked the beginning of vast political, social, and economic changes in those countries that had oil. Governments expanded to include oil ministries, foreign ministries, travel ministries, and others whose purpose was related to oil. Westerners vied for control of the oil industry. In Iraq, for instance, the Iraqi Petroleum Company, shared by British Petroleum, Shell, Mobil, and Standard Oil of New Jersey (Exxon), was established in 1929, and within a few years had a monopoly over Iraqi oil production. Ports like Dubai in the United Arab Emirates were expanded and developed to handle exports. As trading centers, they became

A worker inspects machinery at an oil plant near the Persian Gulf. Over the years, oil has proved to be a source of conflict in the Middle East.

wealthy, modern cities. Those nations without oil could only watch enviously as their oil-rich neighbors became able to afford all the amenities the world had to offer.

Up until the 1970s, Western oil companies largely controlled oil production. They had been given concessions—rights to explore and produce the product—by local rulers who did not fully appreciate the fortune that lay beneath their feet. Concessions usually lasted many years, exempted the company from local taxes, and brought it huge profits. However, with the formation of the Organization of Petroleum Exporting Countries (OPEC) in 1960 and the Organization of Arab Petroleum Exporting Countries (OAPEC) in 1968, Middle Eastern countries began to take more control over their oil. As years passed, most regained control of the industry, thus reaping enormous profits that had once gone to the Western world.

In the 1970s, oil-producing nations realized that oil could be used as a powerful political weapon. Most notable was the oil embargo of 1973–1974, when OPEC announced that its member states would immediately cut oil production by 5 percent and continue to do so each month until Israel withdrew from certain controversial territories it had seized in war. Petroleum-exporting members declared that they would also stop selling oil to the United States until it abandoned its support for Israel. The oil embargo lasted almost half a year and led to long lines at gas stations and sharp increases in the price of fuel (from about $.30 per gallon to about $1.20 per gallon). OPEC lifted the embargo on March 18, 1974, without winning its political demands, but it gained the knowledge and satisfaction that it had economic leverage over the West. The West, on the other hand, realized the implications of having "black gold" concentrated in the hands of a few in this unstable part of the world. The potential for conflict over oil in the future was almost inevitable.

Ports and Waterways

Because the petroleum industry was (and is) so valuable, it was quickly realized that disrupting any aspect of oil production and delivery could be a strategic move in times of war. Not only oil fields, but pipelines, ports, and vessels, necessary to getting oil to market, were vulnerable to attack and could be targeted. Blocking or destroying ports thus became a common tactic during Middle Eastern conflicts. In the 1980 Iran-Iraq War, for instance, both sides bombed each other's tankers, oil facilities, and pipelines as well as the ports of Al Faw in Iraq and Bandar-e Khomeini and Bandar-e Mashur in Iran. The strikes reduced the flow of oil and damaged the other's economy.

Other necessities such as food and heavy equipment also arrived on ships. In countries that had only one port, no access to water could mean strangulation of the economy. In both 1956 and 1967, for example, Egypt blocked the Gulf of Aqaba at the Strait of Tiran, closing a vital shipping corridor for Israel. The strait linked the Israeli port city of Elat to the Red Sea and Israel's major sources of petroleum.

Blocking the Gulf of Aqaba was also important during the Iran-Iraq War, when that waterway was being used as part of a vital supply route for Iraq via Jordan. When the United Nations imposed international sanctions (restrictions) on Iraq and then launched the Persian Gulf War in 1991, the Gulf of Aqaba was again an important blockade point for goods bound for Iraq.

An Ancient Cause of Competition

Water in the Middle East—whether in ports, rivers, or underground aquifers—may be less profitable than oil, but it is another valuable commodity that nations fight over nevertheless. The Middle East has a hot, dry climate. Rain is scant, aquifers (underground water sources) are few, and droughts are recurring. Fast-growing desert populations use water so quickly that supplies cannot be replenished naturally. Agriculture and industry likewise take a huge toll on natural water supplies. Pollution further contributes to a decline in the quality of available water. Maurice Strong, special adviser to the secretary-general of the United Nations, stated in the 1990s: "Water, one of the most ancient causes of competition and conflict, is now emerging as one of the most important sources of potential conflict in the period ahead. . . . Already tensions are rising at the local and regional levels throughout the world over access to water and responsibility for its quality."[22]

A factor that compounds the tension is the fact that all major rivers in the region (with the exception of the Litani River in Lebanon) border or run through at least two countries. The Tigris and Euphrates rivers run through Turkey, Syria, and Iraq. The Jordan River is shared by Jordan, Syria, Israel, and Lebanon. Although relatively small, this river has especially been a source of continual conflict for years.

Beginning about 1949, early Israeli settlers, filled with the dream of reclaiming desert land for farming, began diverting the Jordan's waters to irrigate the Sharon Plain on the coast and the Negev Desert in the south. In 1956, without consulting Syria, Lebanon, or the nation of Jordan (both of which had the right to jointly use the river's waters), Israel expanded its diversion project by building its national water carrier system. This was a combination of open canals, tunnels, reservoirs, and a pipeline that carried water from northern to southern Israel. When Syria tried to stop construction of the system, fighting broke out between the two countries.

Clashes over the Jordan River continued sporadically throughout the next few years. Syria attempted to divert the headwaters away from Israel in the mid-1960s, contributing to tensions that led to the 1967 Arab-Israeli War. During that war, Israel captured the Golan Heights, a narrow mountainous plateau claimed by Syria on Israel's northeastern border. The capture was significant in terms of water sources because the headwaters of the Jordan River and a major aquifer—one of three that supplies Israel's freshwater—originate there.

Even the Golan Heights did not provide adequate water sources for Israel's needs, however. Thus, in the 1960s, the

Desalination

A shortage of water in the Middle East has motivated some countries such as Israel to try desalination—the process of removing salt from ocean water to make it usable. In the following excerpt from "Water, War, and Peace in the Middle East," published in Environment *magazine, Peter H. Gleick, Peter Yolles, and Haleh Hatami identify some pros and cons of the process.*

Ninety-seven percent of the water on the planet is too salty to drink or to grow crops. This has led to great interest in devising ways of removing salt from water in the hope of providing unlimited supplies of freshwater. Indeed, by the beginning of 1990, there were more than 7,500 facilities worldwide producing more than 13.2 million cubic meters of freshwater per day. More than half of this desalination capacity is in the Persian Gulf region, where inexpensive fossil fuels provide the energy necessary to run the plants. For other regions, however, the high energy cost of desalination continues to make unlimited freshwater supplies an elusive goal. In the long run, the use of desalination will be limited by the amount and cost of the energy required to purify saltwater. Unless unanticipated major technical advances reduce overall energy requirements or the price of energy drops substantially, large-scale desalination will always be limited to extremely water-poor and energy-rich nations.

Desalination plants like this one convert salty ocean water into fresh water in some Middle Eastern countries.

nation began experimenting with building desalination (salt-removing) plants that purify saltwater and make it usable for drinking and agriculture. The process remains expensive, so the country continues to rely on aquifers not only in the Golan Heights but in the contested regions of the Gaza Strip and the West Bank. This makes Israel even more reluctant to withdraw from the territories that Palestinians and Syrians claim for themselves. As correspondent Yedidya Atlas notes,

> Withdrawing from [the West Bank]—i.e., the Mountain Aquifer—or from the Golan Heights would create a situation in which the fate of Israel's water supply would be determined by Mr. [Yasser] Arafat's Palestinian Authority and the Syrians, respectively. Can Israel really afford to trust her most valuable and irreplaceable national resource in the hands of those who have had a long history of trying to destroy the Jewish State?[23]

Conflict and Compromise

Water conflicts are not confined to Israel and its neighbors. Tensions have also existed between Syria and Jordan since 1988, when Syria began building twenty-six dams on the Yarmūk River, a tributary of the Jordan. The new construction left the kingdom of Jordan, an already dry nation, with even less water than before. During negotiations in 2001, Syria agreed to give Jordan access to more water, but a breakdown in relations in the future could resurrect the problem.

Similarly, Turkey, Syria, and Iraq have long had conflicts with one another over the Tigris and Euphrates rivers. Disputes arose in the 1960s over how much water each country should be allotted for use. All have growing populations and plan to use more water for irrigation in the future. Turkey and Syria were able to reach an agreement in the 1970s, and cooperated on the construction of several dams. However, their agreement reduced the flow of water to Iraq, which threatened to bomb the dams and even massed troops along the border in 1974. Confrontation ended after Saudi Arabia mediated a peace and Syria agreed to release a fair share of the water to Iraq.

Trouble arose again in 1990 when Turkey completed construction of the Ataturk Dam and began filling the reservoir behind it, effectively cutting off the flow of the Euphrates River for a month. Both Syria and Iraq protested vigorously, adding that the Turks now had a "water weapon"—that is, they could get their way in disagreements by threatening to deprive Syria and Iraq of water. Turkish president Suleyman Demirel's attitude seemed to validate their fears. He stated, "Neither Syria nor Iraq can lay claim to Turkey's rivers. . . . We have a right to do anything we like. The water resources are Turkey's, the oil resources are theirs. We don't say we share the oil resources, and they cannot say they share our water resources."[24]

Border Disputes

Disputes over water and oil have often led to larger border disputes in the Middle

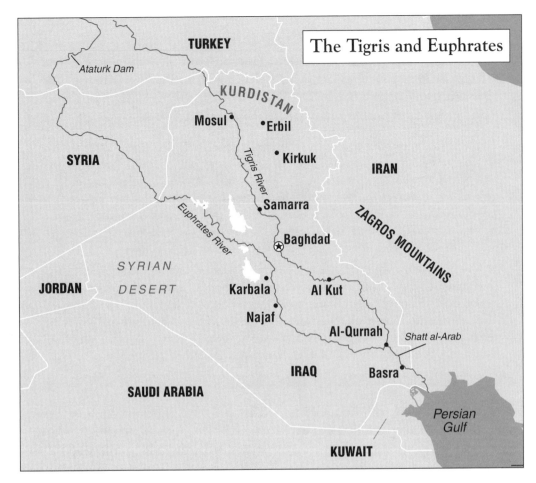

The Tigris and Euphrates

TURKEY

Ataturk Dam

KURDISTAN

Mosul • Erbil

SYRIA

Kirkuk

IRAN

Tigris River

Samarra

Euphrates River

ZAGROS MOUNTAINS

Baghdad

SYRIAN DESERT

JORDAN

Karbala

Al Kut

Najaf

Al-Qurnah

Shatt al-Arab

IRAQ

Basra

SAUDI ARABIA

Persian Gulf

KUWAIT

East. The 1990–1991 Persian Gulf War, for instance, was fought after Iraq invaded oil-rich Kuwait, its southern neighbor. Iraq initially wanted to stop Kuwait from driving up oil prices, but quickly sought to annex the country entirely. Saddam Hussein claimed that the nation belonged to modern-day Iraq because Kuwait had been a part of Iraq during Ottoman times. "The British drew the frontiers separating Kuwait from the new mandate state of Iraq, unwittingly laying the groundwork for future controversies,"[25] states historian William Cleveland.

The Iran-Iraq War was another conflict fought in part over a border dispute, this one involving water and the Shatt al Arab waterway. The waterway, a 120-mile-long stretch where the Tigris and Euphrates rivers come together before they flow into the Persian Gulf, is Iraq's only access to the sea and provides a transportation corridor for oil exports and commodity imports for both Iran and Iraq. Leading up to the war, Iraq claimed that the entire watercourse was its territory. Iran, meanwhile, insisted that the official border was an imaginary line, negotiated during a 1975 treaty, running down the middle of the channel. When Saddam Hussein invaded Iran in 1980, one of his goals was to reverse the 1975

Water Politics

Saudi Arabia's attempt to find answers to its water problems may lead to more political conflict in the Persian Gulf, as Ilan Berman and Paul Michael Wihbey point out in the following excerpt from their article "The New Water Politics of the Middle East," found on the Institute for Advanced Strategic and Political Studies Web site.

Saudi Arabia is another country rapidly approaching a dramatic crisis over water. In Saudi Arabia's case, however, the crisis stems from the country's lack of rivers and permanent bodies of water, as a result of which it relies heavily upon underground water sources for its agricultural and potable [drinkable] water supply. At present, 90% of Saudi Arabia's non-renewable deep-well water is utilized for agricultural purposes. These resources, already precariously low, have been significantly eroded in recent years as a consequence of the Persian Gulf conflict. . . .

Consequently, Saudi Arabia has begun to seek other water sources, a focus that has had pronounced effects on the region. Saudi Arabia's extensive exploration into the underground aquifers in its Eastern Province has reduced the agriculture and water availability of Qatar and Bahrain. The resulting political tension points to an emerging conflict over water resources in the Persian Gulf Peninsula, one that may engulf both Saudi Arabia and her neighbors.

border settlement; indeed, when the war ended in 1988, Iraq controlled the waterway.

Some boundary disagreements, although potentially serious, have been able to be settled without outright war. On the Arabian Peninsula, a treaty was worked out in 1981 that ended a long-term border dispute between Oman and the United Arab Emirates. In 1991 Oman and Saudi Arabia signed a treaty ending a long-standing territorial dispute over the al-Buraymi Oasis, an oil-producing region. In 2000 and 2001, conflicts between Saudi Arabia and Yemen, Saudi Arabia and Qatar, and Qatar and Bahrain concerning the exact location of mutual borders were also settled without violence. The success of such diplomacy made leaders optimistic that peaceful relations could be maintained in the future. "Settling border disputes will definitely be followed by better cooperation not only by the leaders but also by all peoples,"[26] Prince Saud al-Faisal, foreign minister of Saudi Arabia, said in March 2001.

Pan-Arabism

Although disputes over borders have involved natural resources, not all do. Some Middle Eastern leaders have been motivated by power as they tried to erase Western-drawn boundaries and enlarge their nations. Some wanted to assimilate ethnic or religious groups that were once a part of their region. Like Saddam, most discovered that the effort was more difficult than they imagined. Leaders of even the smallest Middle Eastern state had no intention of allowing themselves to be pushed out of power without a struggle. Western nations have usually defended them, wary of any change to the existing conditions for fear it could affect their national interests.

Gamal Abdel Nasser, president of Egypt from 1956 to 1970, was the most significant and successful when it came to actually enlarging the scope of his power beyond borders. Even then, however, his success was short lived. Nasser became very popular after reclaiming the Suez Canal in Egypt from the British. He also initiated farm reforms and other economic policies that lifted the majority of Egyptians out of poverty. While improving his country, Nasser also dreamed of Pan-Arabism—the formation of an association of Arab states that would be unified, strong, and independent of the rest of the world. "Gamal Abd al-Nasser devoted his life to the glory of the Arab nation and its unity and dignity,"[27] declared Palestinian leader Yasir Arafat after Nasser's death in September 1970.

Most Middle Eastern leaders viewed Nasser's dream with skepticism, but Syria agreed and on February 1, 1958, the two countries became one: the United Arab Republic (UAR). The capital of the new nation was Cairo, Egypt, and Nasser became its first president. At first, Syrians wondered why no other country followed them into the union, but when Egyptian military and technical advisers moved in to their country and began treating it as a colony, they understood. There were other irritations as well, such as being ruled from distant Cairo. Syrian UAR leaders were required to live there, and

as a result felt disconnected from their homeland. The union effectively came to an end after a 1961 coup changed Syria's leadership. With the death of Nasser in 1970, the United Arab Republic and his dream of Arab unity faded into history.

Greater Syria

Syria's willingness to unite with Egypt in 1958 demonstrated that it, too, had hopes of redrawing its boundaries and extending its power. Syria has long dreamt of a "Greater Syria," which would ideally encompass Syria, Jordan, Israel, and Lebanon as well as the West Bank and Gaza Strip. This idea dates back to Ottoman times and before, when the region was one administrative area. That dream of unity persists to the present, at least on the part of the Syrian government.

When Hafez al-Assad became president of Syria in 1971, he was determined to make Syria a force to be reckoned with in the Middle East. He made no secret of his intentions as he looked toward his neighbors and began claiming, "We and Lebanon are one country," "We and Palestine form one entity," and "We and Jordan are one country."[28]

To this end, Syrian tanks swept into Jordan in 1970 and began taking over sections of the country. The Jordanians were able to drive them back and preserve the integrity of their nation. Thwarted in his efforts, Assad continued to declare the Jordanian monarchy illegitimate. Speaking through his foreign minister Abd al-Halim Khaddam, he stated in 1981 that "the Jordanian people were always a part of us, and they will always remain so."[29]

Egypt's Champion

A leader of the pan-Arab movement and a champion of Egyptian nationalism, Gamal Abdel Nasser understood how to achieve his political ends, as the following excerpt from the article "Nasserist Rule," found on the Internet at Arab Net, explains.

Gamal Abd-Al Nasser was a charismatic and brilliant political leader who achieved unprecedented popularity both in Egypt and throughout the Arab world. . . . [His] relations with the West were complex, however. He knew that he could never develop Egypt without large infusions of foreign aid and he knew that the West was the most reliable source of this aid. Yet he came to discover that the more anti-Western his stance appeared to be, the more foreign aid he was offered by Western countries to buy his moderation. When at one point in his regime he became more conciliatory to the West, his foreign aid dropped dramatically. As a founding-leader of the Non-aligned movement [tied with neither the Soviets nor the West], Nasser could have it both ways. Along with India's [Jawaharlal] Nehru and Indonesia's Sukarno, Gamal Abd-Al Nasser became a major international power-broker in the politics of the developing world.

The defeat of the Egyptian army and the loss of Sinai [in the 1967 Arab-Israeli War] would have destroyed the political career of an Arab leader of lesser stature and indeed, Abd-Al Nasser offered to resign as president. Such was his extraordinary popularity that the Egyptian people staged massive spontaneous demonstrations in support of the president and he remained in power. His death in 1970 of a heart attack sent shock waves throughout the Arab world. In a stunning display of emotion, millions of Egyptians followed his funeral procession through the streets of Cairo.

Gamal Abdel Nasser championed Egyptian nationalism and the pan-Arab movement.

Assad's attention also focused on Lebanon, where the possibilities for a power play looked brighter. In 1976 the United Nations had authorized the Syrian military to become a mediator in the Lebanese Civil War. Tens of thousands of Syrian troops had marched into Lebanon, where they helped bring about peace between warring parties. Even after the war ended, they remained, and in 1991 the Syrian-Lebanese Treaty of Brotherhood, Cooperation, and Coordination made their presence official. The agreement stated that Syria would continue to en-sure Lebanon's "sovereignty and inde-pendence." However, Syrian defense min-ister Mustafa Tlas gave a hint of the coun-try's real intentions for domination when he stated that "unity" between the two countries would be "soon, or at least in our generation."[30] His words indicated that, although some headway has been made in disputes over boundaries and re-sources, the desire for land—and the wealth and power that comes with it—will continue to pit neighbor against neighbor in the Middle East for years to come.

CHAPTER 4

The Struggle to Rule

L eadership in the Middle East is as diverse as it is difficult. Middle Eastern governments range from dictatorships to democracies, from monarchies ruled by kings to theocracies headed by religious authorities. Leaders over time have been sheikhs, holy men, and street thugs. Some of these have been responsible, while others have been dishonest and self-seeking. Few have enjoyed widespread popular support throughout their entire rule.

There are several reasons for this state of affairs. Some leaders are unpopular because they are repressive and use brutal methods to run their governments. Libyan ruler Muammar Qaddafi is one of them. According to the Congressional Quarterly, "Hundreds of Libyans have reportedly been executed during the . . . decades of [Qaddafi's] rule, and thousands continue to be held as political prisoners. Political parties remain banned, and there is no legal mechanism for political activity other than that controlled by the government."[31]

Some governments are unpopular because of the way they have dealt with the enormous wealth that came with the discovery of oil. For instance, they have tried to modernize, and this has brought criticism from conservative Muslims who see modern ways as evil. Or they have allowed unevenly distributed wealth, corruption, and reckless extravagance in their regimes and have thus earned the resentment of the poor. Some have had to take stern measures to maintain order or counter the threat of overthrow or assassination and have thus earned the dislike of those who value democracy.

Progressive States

With all its complexity, the Middle East would benefit from the best rulers, the most forward-thinking leaders. Instead, even leaders who see themselves as progressive and responsive to their citizens are often conservative and conventional. Leadership in modern times has commonly been confined to a few powerful members of an elite family. Sometimes control has been in the hands of a military man with strong armies at his beck and call. Even if these leaders are responsible, they are likely to follow traditional procedures to protect the status quo. They are also likely to follow Islamic law to some extent, because Muslim beliefs pervade every aspect of the culture. Religion and state are seldom separate, and anyone who does not profess allegiance to God, the Koran, and sharia (religious law) is unlikely to rise to or stay in power.

Egypt, seen by many as the political center of the Arab world, is a good example of a progressive Middle Eastern

Libya's Muammar Qaddafi was known for his brutal and repressive government.

Facing West

Mustafa Kemal, the founder of Turkey, was a benevolent dictator who believed that future prosperity lay in creating a modern, Westernized nation. In A Concise History of the Middle East, *Arthur Goldschmidt Jr. describes how Kemal began shaping Turkey into the unique state that it is today.*

Mustafa Kemal shaped Turkey into a modern, secular nation.

Mustafa Kemal devoted the last fifteen years of his life to changing Turkey from the bastion of Islam into a secular nation-state. Islam, the way of life and basis of government for the Turks since their conversion a thousand years ago, was now to be replaced by Western ways of civilization, justice, and administration. If persuasion failed, then the changes would be effected by force. Twice opposition parties arose within the Grand National Assembly, but in neither case did Kemal let them survive. A Kurdish uprising in 1925 was severely put down, and an attempt on Kemal's life led to the public hanging of most of his political opponents. . . . Kemal admired democracy in the abstract, but he ruled as a stern father and teacher of his people, who he felt were not yet ready to govern themselves democratically. . . .

Turkey faced west [that is, was influenced by Western ideas] in other ways. The Ottoman financial calendar was replaced by the Gregorian one, and clocks were set to European time, a change from the Muslim system by which the date changed at sunset. Metric weights and measures replaced the customary Turkish ones, and the adoption of a formal day of rest (initially Friday, later Sunday) showed how Western the country had become.

nation. It is a republic with a constitution and an elected president. Opposition parties are free to criticize the government, and women have the right to vote. Nevertheless, behavior that conflicts with sharia is prohibited by law. For instance, Muslim women are not permitted to marry Christian men, and homosexuality—condemned in the Koran—can lead to imprisonment and torture. Despite the election process, the president has the right to rule by decree when he is granted emergency powers, and Muhammad Hosni Mubarak has taken advantage of such powers since the assassination of President Anwar Sadat in 1981. Mona Makram Ebeid, a professor of political science at American University at Cairo, speaks of "Egypt's continued experiment with democracy— we can't yet call it democracy."[32]

Turkey, on the other hand, is more truly democratic and Westernized. Its founder, Mustafa Kemal, created a republic parliamentary democracy from the remains of the Ottoman Empire in 1923. He set up secular laws to replace religious ones. Although a dictator, Kemal emphasized modernization, Westernization, and nationalization. He also encouraged equal rights for women and promoted education. After his death in 1938, elections were held and power was transferred peacefully. Corruption and a rise in popularity of Islamic political parties have become threats to the republic's future in the twenty-first century, but the country thus far remains a modern, secular state. Western-style clothing is popular. Boys and girls attend school together. And women have the right to vote, get a divorce, and receive alimony.

Israel is perhaps the most progressive nation in the Middle East; it is a democracy with a parliament, a prime minister, and a multitude of parties. Every Israeli citizen has the right to vote, and both liberal and conservative elements of the population have a voice in leadership. Most Israelis have adopted Western styles of living, working, and having fun. Young couples hold hands in public. Women wear bikinis to the beach. Although the Orthodox Jewish faith plays a large role in government at every level, many Israelis express no belief in God. Author Yossi Klein Halevi comments on how the mixture of Orthodox religion and democracy plays out in the nation:

> Depending on the Israeli being asked, the Jewish state is either a stifling theocracy or a hedonistic [pleasure-seeking] society mimicking the worst excesses of the west. It is a country where Orthodox rabbis can deny the right of a religious marriage to a "bastard," defined by the Bible as the offspring of a married woman who conceived with another man. And [at the same time] it is the only country in the Middle East with an annual gay pride parade, attracting tens of thousands of participants.[33]

Sheikhs and Sultans
Except for nations such as Israel, Turkey, and a few others, Middle Eastern governments are monarchies. Saudi Arabia, Jordan, Bahrain, Oman, Kuwait, and Qatar are all ruled by kings, princes, sultans, or

sheikhs. Some of these monarchs, such as Sultan Qaboos bin Said of Oman and Sheikh Hamad bin Khalifa al-Thani of Qatar, govern with a limited constitution, but their rule is primarily by decree and they have the final say in all matters of government. In monarchies, members of the royal family hold principal posts in the government as well.

The Saudi Arabian government is a monarchy that practices Wahhabism, a strict form of Islam. The country is led by King Fahd bin Abdul Aziz, a member of the Saud royal family. His is one of the most restrictive monarchies in the region. Islamic law serves as the country's constitution. Women enjoy few rights and cannot vote or drive a car. Businesses are required to shut down four times a day for prayer. Violation of laws can be met with canings, amputations, and executions, even for people from another country. For instance, Robert Thomas, an Australian medical technician working in Saudi Arabia, was sentenced to three hundred public lashings and sixteen months in prison after his wife was convicted of stealing equipment from a hospital she worked at. Thomas was found guilty by association under the country's laws.

Monarchs can be authoritarian and tolerate little opposition, but many try to be generous to their subjects. Those with vast oil wealth have taken steps to modernize and provide benefits such as health care, housing, education, and pensions for citizens. Some have yielded to demands to grant women limited rights. For instance, in Qatar, women are allowed to drive if they obtain permits, and female visitors to Qatar need not wear a veil in public.

Even in those countries that seem liberal, however, monarchs remain conservative. For instance, in Kuwait, a monarchy with a constitution, elections, and other elements of democracy, qualifications for voting are so restrictive that only 5 percent of Kuwaitis qualify to cast a ballot. Women, immigrants, the illiterate, and everyone under the age of twenty-one are ineligible. Such restrictions often spark resentment among the people. "It's only a democracy of the few,"[34] says Massoumah al-Mubarak, a professor of international relations and a prominent women's activist. In Jordan, where women have the vote and freer speech is tolerated, activists can still be arrested simply for expressing their views. For instance, Toujan Faisal, Jordan's first female member of parliament, was imprisoned after she accused the prime minister of raising car-insurance rates to benefit his family's insurance business.

Abuse of Power

With so much authority, Middle Eastern leaders can easily abuse their power, and some of them have. For instance, in Oman, Sheikh Said bin Taymur maintained repressive control over his subjects throughout the 1960s, restricting education and banning such innocent items as sunglasses. During the late 1980s and early 1990s, the economy of Qatar was crippled when Emir Sheikh Hamad bin Khalifa al-Thani continuously used petroleum revenues for his own personal use.

In some countries, leaders became ruthless dictators. Such was the case in

Push Toward Democracy

Some Middle Eastern monarchs such as Oman's Sultan Qaboos bin Said are interested in modifying their governments to be more democratic. In 1997 correspondent Judith Miller interviewed Qaboos in Oman. This excerpt from her article "Creating Modern Oman: An Interview with Sultan Qabus" can be found on the Foreign Affairs *Web site.*

The country is in the midst of another dramatic change. Oman is opening up—discreetly as usual. The sultan has convened a Majlis al-Shura, or Consultative Council, a partially elected parliament, which includes the only two women holding elected office in the Gulf region. Last November he unveiled a revolutionary Basic Law, in effect an Islam-based constitution, complete with a bill of rights that guarantees freedom of the press, religious tolerance, and equality of race and gender under law—unprecedented in its comprehensiveness in the conservative Gulf. Oman has no political prisoners, a rarity in the region. And it has a long tradition of religious tolerance, due in part to its Ibadhi sect's interpretation of Islam. The sultan himself has allocated land for Western churches and Hindu temples. It seems clear that he intends to move toward representative government and the rule of law, but at a measured pace, when his people are ready. "You can't push things too far or too fast in the Gulf," he told me in flawless English during a three-hour interview at his palace in Muscat in February.

Sultan Qaboos bin Said hopes to bring democracy to Oman.

Iraq, where Saddam Hussein opted to crush his opposition and use stern, repressive means to control unrest in the general population.

Since his entry into politics at the age of nineteen, Saddam had been a violent man. He was part of a 1959 assassination attempt against Iraqi prime minister Abdul Karim Kassem. In 1968 he helped lead the revolt that finally brought the Baath Party to power under General Ahmed Hassan al-Bakr. Given the post of vice president, Saddam built an elaborate network of secret police to root out dissidents, threatening or killing anyone who disagreed with Bakr. In 1978 he ordered the deaths of seven thousand people alleged to be Communists. He also deposed Bakr on July 16, 1979, and assumed the office of president of Iraq himself.

Shortly after taking office, in order to crush any opposition, Saddam had at least 450 of Iraq's most prominent men put to death, including union leaders, financiers, army officers, lawyers, judges, journalists, editors, professors, religious leaders, and leaders of most of the smaller parties and ethnic groups. The most overt violence was justified in the name of national security. When asked by a journalist if his police were guilty of torturing and killing his opponents, Saddam responded, "Of course. What do you expect if they [the challengers] oppose the regime?"[35]

In the early 1980s, Saddam used chemical weapons to crush a Kurdish rebellion in northern Iraq, leaving fifteen thousand Kurds dead. Revelations in 2003 showed that the dictator may have had more than three hundred thousand of his opponents and their families killed between 1983 and 1991. U.S. official Sandra Hodgkinson stated in late 2003,

> We have found mass graves of women and children with bullet holes in their heads, and we have found mass graves of husbands and fathers out in the desert where they were buried. We met survivors who crawled out of mass graves after being buried alive. We met with families whose loved ones did not escape.[36]

Coups and Revolutions

It took U.S. might to topple Saddam Hussein from power, but other unpopular government leaders have been removed by their own people through coups, revolutions, civil wars, and assassinations.

Coups have been common, particularly in those nations where governments are regarded as illegitimate and unrest is just below the surface. On occasion, the power shifts are led by the military, and are greeted with relief if the populace has suffered under a particularly repressive regime. Most of the time, however, the takeovers are deplored as lawless events that make life unstable. They are seen as taking place with little regard for what ordinary people want, and because of such public attitudes, they have a negative influence on the legitimacy of the new government that takes power.

In Iraq between 1958 and 1968, four coups and several other assaults on the government took place. Syria, which has a reputation as the Arab state most prone to military coups, went through at least six successful or attempted government overthrows plus multiple changes of government leaders between 1961 and 1970. President Hafez al-Assad, who brought stability to the government during his nearly three-decade rule from 1971 to 2000, came to power as part of a coup. Although he led Syria until his death, his rule was repressive and he lacked the respect an elected leader might have claimed.

Some overthrows take place in apparently stable governments, as was the case in Iran in 1979. Mohammad Reza Shah Pahlavi ascended the throne of Iran in

Saddam Hussein greets a crowd of Iraqis in 1998. During his years in power, Hussein threatened or killed anyone who opposed him.

1941, and in 1963 instituted a reform program with U.S. assistance. It included land redistribution among citizens, extensive construction, the promotion of literacy, and the emancipation of women.

Despite his reforms and his years in office, however, the shah faced growing criticism. Ordinary Iranians were increasingly unhappy as oil wealth was unequally distributed. As popular discontent grew, the shah became more repressive, calling on his brutal secret police to put down domestic strife. The country became a police state complete with informers, censorship, arbitrary arrest, imprisonment, and widespread torture.

The Ayatollah Ruhollah Khomeini waves to supporters. In 1979, Khomeini led a violent coup that overthrew the government and established Islamic law in Iran.

The United States chose to ignore the flaws in the shah's leadership. It regarded him as an ally who would guard against Communist intrusion into the Middle East. Because of his power and its backing, it believed his regime was stable. Thus, the United States was suprised when, in the spring of 1979, the Iranian people rebelled. Led by the Ayatollah Ruhollah Khomeini, an Islamic cleric, they forced the shah into exile. They then voted to establish a new government with the ayatollah as its head. Strict Islamic law was enforced, women were ordered to wear veils, and religious courts replaced the former criminal justice system. Milton Viorst writes,

> Proving himself as ruthless as the Shah had been, [Khomeini] had thousands killed while stamping out a rebellion of the secular left. He stacked the state bureaucracies with faithful clerics and drenched the schools and the media with his personal doctrines. After purging the military and security services, he rebuilt them to ensure their loyalty to the clerical state.[37]

Although the Iranian theocracy has existed to the present, it is not immune to violence and may be a hot spot in the Middle East in the future. Citizens have come to realize that strict Islamic law is oppressive and does not promote modernization, a strong economy, or comfortable lifestyles. They have again begun to demand change. An election in 2000 put reformer Mohammad Khatami into the presidency, but other religious leaders still use gangs of zealous young Muslims to intimidate the population into leading an ultraconservative lifestyle. In the future, such repression may again explode into another period of bloodshed. "[The Khatami-led reform movement] is popular, but God knows what they are going to do," said Asrar Raesi, an Iranian shopkeeper. "I'm afraid we're going to have another revolution."[38]

Civil War and Assassination

Coups are only one of the ways that disgruntled citizens in the Middle East effect change in their nations. Some choose paths that lead their country into civil war, such as the one that literally tore the country of Lebanon apart from 1975 until 1990.

Another civil war took place in Jordan in 1970, after Palestinian and Jordanian guerrilla organizations began attempting to overthrow the king, calling for a general strike of the Jordanian population, and organizing civil disobedience campaigns. Their goal was to make Jordan into a Palestinian state, to which they dreamed of adding Israel.

In September 1970, King Hussein bin Talal, who had at first tried compromise, decided it was time to act. He directed the Jordanian military to launch attacks to defeat the guerrillas and push them out of the country. During the fighting, thousands of insurgents and Palestinian civilians were killed. The war became known as "Black September," and the king's eventual victory cemented his position as Jordan's rightful leader. Author Judith Miller observes, "Hussein had not sought this test of wills. He had done everything possible

Palestinian guerrillas patrol a Jordanian street during the 1970 civil war. Jordan's king proved victorious in that conflict and cemented his position as the country's rightful leader.

to avoid it. But after Black September, the king's legitimacy in the East Bank [Jordan] was never again challenged."[39]

Coups, revolutions, and civil wars have been outlets for groups who are dissatisfied with the government status quo. In-

dividuals who are frustrated, impatient, or angry, however, have sometimes turned to assassination in an attempt to bring about change. Virtually no country in the Middle East has been immune to the problem in recent decades, and those who have been killed were often responsible men who truly wanted to bring peace or prosperity to their country.

In 1951, for instance, a religious fanatic killed Iranian premier General Ali Razmara because he supported U.S.-suggested economic reforms. That same year, on July 20, a Palestinian extremist assassinated Jordan's King Abdullah bin al-Hussein out of fear that the king would make peace with Israel. Hussein bin Talal, Abdullah's grandson, was at his grandfather's side and was himself shot and almost killed.

The assassinations continued during the 1970s and 1980s. In November 1971, Jordanian prime minister Wasfi Tal was killed in Cairo, Egypt, by a band of Palestinian insurgents in revenge for his efforts against them in the Jordanian Civil War. In August 1981 in Iran, radical political opponents of President Mohammad Ali Rajai and Prime Minister Mohammad Javad Bahonar bombed the two men's offices, killing both just weeks after they took office. In September 1982, Bashir Gemayel, who had been elected president of Lebanon on August 23, 1982, was killed when his political party's office was bombed.

Perhaps two of the most notable assassinations in the region were those of President Anwar Sadat of Egypt in 1981 and Prime Minister Yitzhak Rabin of Israel in 1995. Sadat had won the Nobel Peace Prize with Israeli prime minister Menachem Begin after the two made notable efforts to promote peace between their two countries in 1978. On October 6, 1981, Sadat was shot down in Cairo by a religious extremist opposed to his peacemaking. Rabin, who was awarded

History Repeats Itself

The assassination of Yitzhak Rabin on November 4, 1995, brought back painful memories of Anwar Sadat's violent death in 1981. In an article found on the CNN Web site, correspondent Gayle Young describes the sadness Egyptians felt on the day of Rabin's funeral.

For many Egyptians, the funeral of Israeli Prime Minister Yitzhak Rabin Monday was all too familiar. In 1981, Egyptian President Anwar Sadat was assassinated. Like Rabin, he was killed at a public function by religious extremists opposed to his Nobel Prize-winning efforts to promote peace in the Middle East.

Normally rather cool toward Israel, Egyptians expressed empathy for their Jewish neighbors Monday. "This is like the day Sadat died," said an Egyptian man. "Rabin was a man of peace, and we feel very sad." "It is a fate that we didn't want for Sadat and we didn't want for Rabin," said an Egyptian woman. . . .

Several years ago, Rabin visited Sadat's tomb. Now both men have become symbols, some would say martyrs to the same cause. In this ancient land it is perhaps no surprise that history tends to repeat itself.

the Nobel Peace Prize in 1994 for his efforts to bring peace to the Middle East, was shot at a peace rally in Tel Aviv, Israel, on November 4, 1995, by a right-wing Jewish law student who was angry because Rabin wanted "to give our country to the Arabs."[40]

With emotions so charged, debates over leadership are likely to remain tense, even explosive, in the Middle East. When even the most responsible leaders are thwarted while trying to carry out their aims, the chance of peaceful compromise seems slim. Not surprisingly, many people in the Middle East get discouraged and feel that no one really wants to find answers. In the words of one Israeli child, "Sometimes I get the feeling that some people don't really want peace, they just want to fight . . . and win."[41]

CHAPTER 5

Clash over Palestine

Among the many conflicts besetting the Middle East, those over the nation of Israel, and the territories known as the West Bank and Gaza Strip, have been the most polarizing—and the most discouraging to peacemakers—over time. Issues such as refugees, settlements, and security barriers inflame tempers and provoke violence. Nevertheless, most problems can be traced back to a primary one: who owns the land. The borders of the region once known as Palestine were not clearly defined, and both Jews and Palestinians believe they are the legitimate owners. Neither side wants to concede that the other may have rights in the area. Former U.S. president Jimmy Carter, who spent much of his presidency trying to solve the Palestinian conflict, observes, "Each side fears total destruction or complete denial by the other, this worry be-

ing fed by a history of violence and hatred."[42]

The Zionist Movement

The conflict over Palestine was unwittingly started by Theodor Herzl, a Jewish lawyer and journalist from Hungary. In the late 1800s he began dreaming of a homeland for Jews who had been scattered throughout the world for centuries. In all of these places, Jews had been persecuted, resented, and often killed. Herzl had experienced anti-Semitism (hatred of Jews) firsthand while working in France and decided that Jews would be safe and free only when they had a nation of their own. He spent his life making his dream a reality. His statement "If you will it, it is not a dream"[43] became the motto of Zionism, the international movement for Jews to establish a homeland in Palestine, which they considered their biblical/ancestral homeland.

When the British became administrators of Palestine at the end of World War I, it served their interests to give some support to the Zionist movement. Many Zionist Jews were prosperous Europeans who would make valuable allies in the Middle East. On November 2, 1917, British foreign minister Lord Arthur James Balfour made that support official when he issued the following statement: "His Majesty's Government views with favor the establishment in Palestine of a national home for the Jewish people, and will use their best endeavors to facilitate the achievement of this object."[44]

Despite this statement, over the next few decades, British backing swung between Jews and the Arabs who also lived in Palestine. Jewish immigration to Palestine was not stopped, but it was discour-

Jewish immigrants work a farm in Palestine. During the early twentieth century, many Jews moved to Palestine in hope of establishing a safe and permanent homeland.

The Arab League

The League of Arab States, also known as the Arab League, was formed almost sixty years ago with the goal to serve the common good, ensure better conditions, guarantee the future, and fulfill the hopes and expectations of all Arab countries. Author Ahmed Janabi gives a brief overview of the organization in his article "The Arab League: Fifty-nine Years On," published on the Aljazeera.net Web site.

"[In] March 1945 representatives from Egypt, Syria, Iraq, Lebanon, Transjordan (now Jordan), Saudi Arabia and Yemen signed the Arab League accord in Cairo. The league was established to promote economic development, settle disputes between Arab countries, and coordinate political aims.

Over the years 15 other Arab countries joined the league, the last one was the Comoros in 1993, increasing the number of member states to the present 22. . . . Despite Jordanian objections, in 1964 the Arab League admitted the Palestinian Liberation Organisation as the representative of all Palestinians.

The league received a major setback after the signing of the Egypt-Israel peace treaty in March 1979. Conflicts over policy with Israel intensified, eventually the league's headquarters were moved from Cairo, Egypt, to the Tunisian capital of Tunis. Egypt's membership in the Arab League was suspended. Ten years later Egypt's membership was reinstated and the headquarters were moved back to Cairo in 1990."

aged, as were land purchases. Nevertheless, Jewish settlers continued to act as if the land they lived on and sought to buy was theirs. They bought more, displacing the indigenous Arab population as they did so. They built communities. They established homes and families. Israeli military commander and diplomat Moshe Dayan was one of the first settlers born in the region. He remembered:

We came to this country which was already populated by Arabs, and we are establishing a Hebrew, that is a Jewish state here. In considerable areas of the country . . . we bought the lands from the Arabs. Jewish villages were built in the place of Arab villages.

Nahalal (Dayan's own village) arose in the place of Mahalul, Gevat—in the place of Jibta. . . . There is not one place built in this country that did not have a former Arab population. [45]

Born in War

By 1948, Britain's attempts to please both Arab Palestinians and Zionists had only succeeded in angering both groups. In addition, Hitler's mass murder of Jews in Europe during a period known as the Holocaust had motivated hundreds of thousands to flee to Israel, swelling the numbers and making the push for nationhood more intense. Palestinians and their neighbors were ready to go to war to prevent that from happening. Conceding that it could not satisfy everyone, Britain handed the problem to the United Nations. The UN decided to divide the region and retain control of the city of Jerusalem, making it an international city. The Zionists accepted the partition of the region. The Palestinians, claiming that dividing the land was illegal, did not.

On May 14, 1948, the day before the last British soldier left Palestine, Zionist leader David Ben-Gurion formally proclaimed Israel an independent nation. He stated:

> We, the members of the National Council, representing the Jewish people in Palestine and the Zionist movement of the world, met together in solemn assembly today, the day of the termination of the British mandate for Palestine, by virtue of the natural and historic right of the Jewish and of the Resolution of the General Assembly of the United Nations, hereby proclaim the establishment of the Jewish State in Palestine, to be called Israel.[46]

The United States, the Soviet Union, and other countries throughout the world immediately recognized Israel's sovereignty. Egypt, Syria, Jordan, Lebanon, and Iraq, however, believed that the land rightly belonged to Palestinian Arabs. To keep it, all opted for war. Secretary-general of the Arab League, Assam Pasha, expressed Arab intentions: "This will be a war of extermination and a momentous massacre which will be spoken of like the Mongolian massacres and the Crusades."[47]

Outnumbered by their enemies, Jewish fighters fought fiercely, and in the end they controlled more land than they had originally been granted. Egypt, Syria, Jordan, and Lebanon signed armistices (cease-fires) with Israel in 1949, but their humiliation over their failure to destroy Israel was intense. The loss was a source of continual conflict for years to come.

"The Destruction of Israel"

The end of the war for independence was not the beginning of peace in the region. For the next two decades, Israelis fought for their lives in their new homeland. Between 1949 and 1956, Muslim terrorist groups called fedayeen regularly attacked the civilian population. In 1956 Egypt blockaded the port of Elat in an attempt to strangle Israel's economy.

Raids and closures did not work, so Israel's enemies again tried war. In May 1967, Egyptian forces moved in to the Sinai Peninsula while Syrian, Jordanian, Iraqi, and Saudi Arabian troops massed on Israel's borders. President Nasser of Egypt explained the move in blunt terms: "Our basic goal is the destruction of Israel. The Arab people want to fight."[48]

Israel was ready. Before its enemies could strike, it launched its own attack and, in what became known as the Six-Day War, captured the entire Sinai Peninsula, the West Bank, and the Golan Heights. The capture pushed back the enemy, created a buffer zone around the country, and provided Israeli citizens greater protection. Syrians could no longer fire down on Israeli villages and cities from the Golan Heights. Jordanians could no longer easily strike Israel's energy and power installations from the West Bank. In addition, water sources and important religious sites, including Jerusalem and Bethlehem, came under Israeli control.

To recover lost territory, Egypt and Syria launched another attack on Israel on October 6, 1973. Iraqi, Saudi, Kuwaiti, Lebanese, Jordanian, and other military forces also joined the fight. The date was strategically chosen—Yom Kippur, the holiest day of the Jewish calendar. While most Israelis were in synagogues praying and fasting, Egyptian troops and helicopters crossed the Suez Canal and Syrian troops began to attack Israel's installations in the Golan Heights.

Israel was thrown on the defensive during the first two days of fighting. Then, it mobilized its reserves and fought off the invaders. Israeli forces were so successful that they carried the war deep into Syria and Egypt. Hostilities were eventually brought to a halt, but once again, deep-seated anger and resentment set the stage for violence in the future.

The Refugees

Coupled with war, the displacement of hundreds of thousands of Palestinians added to the upheaval that marked Israel's early years. By the end of 1948, over half a million Palestinian men, women, and children had fled their homes in Israel to escape war and to avoid possible acts of vengeance by Israeli soldiers. Most who fled ended up in UN refugee camps near Israel's borders in Syria, the Gaza Strip, southern Lebanon, and Jordan. Arthur Goldschmidt explains: "The Arab countries would not absorb them [grant them citizenship], mainly for political reasons, although some would have found it economically hard to do so. The Palestinians themselves rejected assimilation because they wanted to go back to their homes."[49]

As time passed, the refugees remained in the camps—crude, makeshift places where food and

Israel After the Six-Day War

Beirut

LEBANON
Damascus
SYRIA

GOLAN HEIGHTS

Haifa
Sea of Galilee
Nazareth

Mediterranean Sea

Jordan River

WEST BANK
Amman
Tel Aviv-Jaffa
Ashdod
Jericho
Ashkelon
Jerusalem
Gaza
Hebron
Dead Sea
Gaza Strip

NEGEV DESERT

JORDAN

SINAI PENINSULA
Aqaba

E G Y P T

Gulf of Suez

Gulf of Aqaba

SAUDI ARABIA

Israeli territory 1949–June 10, 1967
Israeli conquests June 5–11, 1967

clothing were scarce and educational and health facilities minimal. Despite the temporary feel of the places, most people went on with their lives, marrying, having children, and eking out a living. Israel's capture of the West Bank and the Gaza Strip in the 1967 war drove more people off the land and added to the crowding. By 2001, over 1 million people were living in fifty-nine camps that

A Palestinian woman and her children live as refugees in a camp along the Israeli border.

To Die as Martyrs

Nidhal is a young Palestinian from the Gaza Strip who has taken part in protests against the Israeli army and seen fellow demonstrators injured and killed. In "Voices from the Conflict," a special report on the Middle East found on the BBC News Web site, he expresses his feelings and the feelings of other angry Palestinians as they fight for a homeland.

Our stones hurt the Jews. When young men confront the Israeli soldiers, they shoot at them, and this draws more young men who come out to help him and to fight for the Aqsa [mosque in Jerusalem] and their land and their friends.

We gather the stones and we use slingshots and slings, which we make, and we try to hit the soldiers. And thanks be to God, good will come of it.

They are armed to the teeth. We put our faith in God and good will come of it. We don't feel any fear. We feel courageous and strong. We would be proud to die as martyrs, and our family would be proud. Martyrs go to heaven to be with God.

I've seen people be killed and get hurt. When this happens, some shout "There is no God but God, and Mohammad is his prophet," and others shout "God is great." This puts the fear in the Jews and they retreat. All the protesters are brave and they are ready to confront the Israeli soldiers, even for a hundred years, to the last drop of blood.

stretched from Syria to Tunisia. Another 2 to 3 million lived as exiles in other countries. Although not recognized as a nation when they were uprooted, they gradually developed a feeling of unity and continued to dream of a return to their original homeland. That dream was fanned by the Palestine Liberation Organization (PLO), a nationalist association created by Egypt, Syria, Jordan, and other countries in 1964 that is dedicated to the establishment of an independent Palestinian state.

The PLO and Terrorism Against Israel

The Palestine Liberation Organization's dream of a Palestinian state hung on the destruction of Israel. Yasir Arafat be-

came the organization's chairman in 1968, and took charge of the army of fighters made up of refugees and Palestinians who lived on the West Bank. The latter were especially dissatisfied because many worked in Israel and were treated as second-class citizens because they were not Jewish.

With the PLO dedicated to their cause, Palestinians decided to begin fighting for what they wanted. At first, they launched random attacks on Israeli police, throwing stones and bottles and an occasional bomb. In 1987 they launched the intifada, an uprising of violence and political conflict. They stepped up bombings and other acts of terror. They built barricades at the entrances of their camps and villages to ward off Israeli efforts to catch lawbreakers. They refused to sell Jewish products in their stores and refused to work for Jewish employers. "It was to show the Israeli public that we are not Israelis," explained Musa al-Kam, a Palestinian lawyer. "If it did not happen . . . , we would be just like Israelis—only without our land and without our Palestinian identities. In twenty more years Palestinians would be without personalities."[50]

Israel responded with force, and the bloodshed escalated. After a second intifada uprising was launched in 2000, riots occurred and suicide bombings became an almost daily occurrence. More than 850 Israelis were killed by such attacks between 2000 and 2003. In the city of Haifa alone, 53 Israelis were blown up by suicide bombers on buses and in restaurants between December 2002 and March 2003. Even increased security could not stop the violence. Police officer Danny Kuffler was a witness to the October 2003 suicide bombing in the Maxim Restaurant in Haifa that took the lives of 19 people. "The restaurant was full," he remembered. "The bomber passed the security guard at the entrance, went inside, turned on the explosive device and all the restaurant exploded."[51]

The Settlement Problem

As time passed, Palestinians modified their dream of regaining all of Israel and focused instead on reclaiming just the West Bank and Gaza Strip. They cited UN Resolution 242—issued in November 1967—as a basis for their ownership claim. The resolution officially set Israel's boundaries outside of the disputed areas and called for a just solution to the refugee problem.

Israel disagreed. It claimed that holding the West Bank and Gaza was necessary if the remainder of the UN resolution was to be recognized. That part called for their right "to live in peace within secure and recognized boundaries."[52] According to Israeli arguments, the West Bank in particular was necessary as a buffer zone against potential aggression from its neighbors.

Israel had another motivation for retaining the West Bank, however. Handing it back to the Palestinians would mean having to uproot Jewish settlers who lived there. These were devout Zionists who saw the region as part of that given to them by God. The establishment of the settlements served as claims to the land. They were letting their enemies know that they were in the region to stay and would not be easily dislodged. By 2003, about 230,000 Israeli settlers lived in 150 settlements on the West Bank.

A poll in 2003 showed that 69 percent of Israelis were willing to abandon the settlements in exchange for peace. Israeli leaders who needed every vote they could get to retain power could not afford to ignore the remaining 31 percent of the population, however. Thus, more settlements continue to be built, even though their presence is divisive and a stumbling block to peace. One Israeli soldier who guards the settlements gave his opinion: "Some day there has to be a peace deal and all these settlements are going to have to come down. Frankly, what we are doing here is useless. We shouldn't be here, and neither should they."[53]

Palestinians agree. They continue to resort to violence to drive settlers off the land. They have also launched suicide bombings inside Israel itself, carried out by willing men and women who hope to shape political policy through intimidation. "The only way out of this [violence] is for the Israelis to withdraw from our towns and villages and for the settlers who weigh so heavy on us to be sent away,"[54] stated Sleiman Mahmoud Shimlawi, a Palestinian farmer in the West Bank village of Haris.

The Fence

As suicide bombings ratcheted up tensions in Israel, the Israeli government decided to take drastic measures. In June 2002, it authorized the construction of a security fence that seperates Israel from

In June 2002, in response to a barrage of suicide bombings, the Israeli government sanctioned the construction of this security fence that seperates Israel from the West Bank.

the West Bank, designed to block the enemy who had been able to slip across Israel's open border in the past. By late 2003, almost eighty miles of concrete, barbed wire, watchtowers, and electronic sensors had been erected. In most places, the line followed that recommended by Resolution 242; in other spots, however, the barricades cut through Palestinian farms and neighborhoods.

Palestinians and others around the world protested the project, claiming it was a hindrance to peace efforts. Israelis insisted it was necessary in the face of uncontrollable violence, and promised that they would remove the barrier when the danger subsided. Critics remained skeptical. "It is a sinful assault on our land, an act of racism and apartheid [segregation] which we totally reject,"[55] declared Yasir Arafat in June 2002. Israel's Consul General Meir Shlomo disagreed. He wrote in December 2003,

Sadly, it is the bleak reality inflicted by Arafat, [and terrorist groups] Hamas and Islamic Jihad that demands the

PLO Leader

Yasir Arafat has been head of the Palestine Liberation Organization for over forty years, and in that time, his public persona has undergone a change. The Internet article "Profile of Yasser Arafat, President of Palestinian Council," found on the ABC News Web site, gives a glimpse of when that change came about.

As a teenager in the 1940s, Arafat became involved in the Palestinian cause. Before the Arabs were defeated by Israel in 1948, Arafat was a leader in the Palestinian effort to smuggle arms into the territory. . . .

In 1956 he founded Al Fatah, an underground terrorist organization. At first Al Fatah was ignored by larger Arab nations such as Egypt, Syria, and Jordan, which had formed their own group—the Palestine Liberation Organization. It wasn't until the 1967 Arab-Israeli War, when the Arabs lost the Gaza Strip, Golan Heights and West Bank, that Arab nations turned to Arafat. In 1968 he became the leader of the PLO.

For two decades the PLO launched bloody attacks on Israel, and Arafat gained a reputation as a ruthless terrorist. But by 1988, when he told the United Nations that the PLO would recognize Israel as a sovereign state, Arafat had warmed to diplomacy. Then in 1993, the unthinkable happened. The terrorist leader, who had rarely been seen without his signature ghutra [head scarf] and scruffy beard, met with his avowed enemies. The secret peace talks in Norway led to the Oslo Peace Accords with Israeli Prime Minister Yitzak Rabin. The agreement granted limited Palestinian self-rule and earned Arafat, Rabin and Israeli Foreign Minister Shimon Peres the 1994 Nobel Peace Prize. In January 1996 Arafat was elected the first president of the Palestinian Council governing the West Bank and Gaza Strip.

construction of a fence. In fact, the security fence could be named "The Arafat Fence" because it is his unrelenting support of terrorist organizations that promotes violence and blocks peace. [56]

Whether Yasir Arafat supports terrorist organizations is a matter of debate, but undoubtedly terrorism is a roadblock to peace in Israel and the Middle East. A relatively few militants, filled with hate, and with nothing to lose, have been able to undo months and years of diplomacy and compromise. Beyond the reach or authority of government leaders, they have inflicted serious damage on peace processes, especially in the twenty-first century. "These criminals have no religion, and they have no human cause," U.S. secretary of state Colin Powell said in 2001. "Their goal, and the goal of all like them, is to divide and embitter people. . . . [But] it is time—no, it is past time—to end this terrible toll on the future. It is time—past time—to bring the violence to an end and to seek a better day." [57]

CHAPTER 6

Terrorism and the Middle East

There have always been those who believe that the only way to solve problems in the Middle East is by using violence. Most have political goals, such as the establishment of fundamentalist Islamic governments or the creation of a Palestinian state, and believe them to be unattainable through peaceful means. Some are mentally unstable or are searching for attention or notoriety. Some are poor, angry, and ready to blame those who are better off. Some have embraced a radical form of religion that makes them feel they are pleasing God when they strike out at unbelievers. The young are particularly prone to adopt such viewpoints, as historian Thomas Friedman observes: "Young urban poor are economically, socially, and psychologically vulnerable to promises of the millennium [a time of joy and prosperity], to the in-toxication of sacred religious texts or to the illusion of a quick fix."[58]

As Friedman notes, poverty and lack of opportunity are strong motivators for terrorists, especially when they see and hear about the affluence of the Western world on television and radio every day. In the case of Palestinians, they have only to look at nearby Jewish neighborhoods to find people that are better off socially and economically. The conditions in which they are trapped—often through no fault of their own—are depressing, and with nothing to lose, they lash out against those they blame for their troubles.

In recent times, suicide bombing has become the most successful weapon in the terrorists' arsenal. Suicide bombers are usually deeply religious people who believe God will bless them for sacrificing their lives in defense of Islam. Because they have no desire to escape death, they are willing to carry explosives into the heart of a crowd and then detonate them to create the greatest amount of devastation.

Terrorist groups regularly use suicide bombings to sow chaos, kill and demoralize, and block any compromise efforts with their enemies. They also value terrorism for its shock value, and for the fact that it is almost impossible to combat. Stopping an enemy who is willing to die for a cause is a nearly insurmountable task, as Thomas Friedman observes: "When you have large numbers of people ready to commit suicide, and ready to do it by making themselves into human bombs, using the most normal instruments of

Israelis clean up after a suicide bomb attack on a Jerusalem bus. Suicide bombs have become the weapon of choice for Palestinian terrorists.

daily life—an airplane, a car, a garage door opener, a cell phone, fertilizer, a tennis shoe—you create a weapon that is undeterrable, undetectable and inexhaustible."[59]

The Fundamentalists

Most Middle Eastern terrorist groups are composed of individuals known as fundamentalists—those who use violence to further a cause and misuse Islam to attract followers. Whereas moderate or secular Muslims express their religion by following the spirit rather than the letter of Islamic law—that is, by living an ethical life, rejecting intimidation and violence, and making godly decisions even in the midst of modern societies in which they live—fundamentalist Muslims emphasize that every verse in the Koran should be followed to the letter. "They go to the Koran and say, 'What did the prophet [Muhammad] say or do?'" said Dr. Richard Antoun, a professor of anthropology at Binghamton University in New York. "They go back to the original time as a model for all time. . . . In a sense, you're erasing history."[60] Fundamentalists also tend to focus on scriptures that serve their purpose and use extreme interpretations to make their points. For instance, the term *jihad*, which literally means "to struggle," is interpreted as "holy war" by fundamentalists. More moderate Muslims define the term as a person's internal struggle with sin and, rarely, the defense of a Muslim homeland when it is attacked.

Fundamentalists acknowledge no law but sharia—Muslim law—which is conservative and sometimes harsh. They be-lieve that Islamic societies should be theocracies, not democracies. Their interpretation of sharia leads them to ignore human rights, reject people of different faiths, and scorn the liberal principles of modern society. They also justify terrorism through sharia and jihad. "[Fundmentalist] statements on jihad not only argue the justifications for going to war against Western enemies, but also justify terrorism and individual acts of violence against the enemy, civilian or otherwise, wherever they may be found in the world," states Abdulaziz Sachedina, professor of Islamic studies at the University of Virginia. "[However,] this argument for terrorism as a legitimate means of conduct in war is a clear departure from the classical rulings which regard the ethics of war as an important part of jihad."[61]

Palestinian Terrorism

A long list of Muslim fundamentalist terrorist groups exist in the Middle East today. Many have as their goal the destruction of Israel and the establishment of a Palestinian state. In the event that Israel is not destroyed, they demand that the West Bank and Gaza Strip be turned over to the Palestinians. In their opinion, Israelis have seized land that rightfully belongs to the Palestinian people. Recognition of the Jewish nation is unacceptable, and they do their best to undermine anyone's efforts to establish a peaceful relationship with it.

Three of the most notorious groups in recent years are Hamas (Islamic Resistance Movement), the Palestine Liberation Front, and the Al-Aqsa Martyrs Brigade, all of which primarily carry out

Difficult Problems

The roots of terrorism lay in the deep frustration that drives many young Middle Eastern men and women to violence. As R. Stephen Humphreys explains in the following excerpt from his book Between Memory and Desire: The Middle East in a Troubled Age, *a growing youth population, economic stagnation, and a lack of opportunity compound the problem.*

The first thing one needs to know about the contemporary Middle East is that the average age of the population is about sixteen—half the average age in the United States. That one fact tells volumes about the intractable problems confronting the governments of the region, and why their record in solving these problems is such a spotty one. To begin with, it means that the majority of the population (taking both the very young and the aged) is a consumer of expensive services, especially education, housing, food, and medical care, while producing little wealth. It also means that the labor markets are flooded with young adults, increasingly well educated and equipped to participate in a modern economy, but also increasingly frustrated in their efforts to get even a low-paying entry-level job. . . .

On a different level, young people everywhere are impatient with authority and in search of meaning for their lives—hence the magnetism of ideologies that explain and solve everything. When two-thirds of the population is less than twenty-five, the search for meaning and alienation from the stifling established order inevitably become a defining element of the whole society.

attacks on Israelis. The Al-Aqsa Martyrs Brigade is a group of West Bank militias that have ties to Yasir Arafat, and that have been one of the driving forces behind the second Palestinian intifada. "We are committed to the continuation of the resistance and the struggle against the occupation of all of Palestine," the group stated in November 2003. "We swear there will be more revenge, more suicide attacks, we will avenge the blood of our martyrs, we will put an end to the occupation [of Palestine]."[62]

The Abu Nidal Organization (ANO), which split from the PLO in 1974, also targets Israelis, but has also carried out terrorist attacks in twenty other countries throughout the world. Hezbollah—the Party of God—is a Lebanon-based group that takes its ideological inspiration from the teachings of the late Ayatollah Khomeini. Its efforts to eliminate Israel and establish Palestinian rule in Lebanon have been marked by the suicide truck bombings of the U.S. embassy and U.S. Marine barracks in Beirut in October 1983 and the U.S. embassy annex in Beirut in September 1984. Elements of Hezbollah were also responsible for the kidnapping and detention of U.S. citizens and other Westerners in Lebanon in the 1980s.

Al Qaeda

Overarching almost all terrorist groups is al Qaeda, the complex, multilevel terrorist organization established in 1988 by

Osama bin Laden heads al Qaeda, the world's largest and most complex terrorist network.

Saudi millionaire Osama bin Laden. One of its primary goals is to drive Americans and American influence out of all Muslim nations, particularly Saudi Arabia. Bin Laden believes the country, the birthplace of Islam, is defiled by the American presence. He explained in 1998:

> The call to wage war against America was made because America has spear-headed the crusade against the Islamic nation, sending tens of thousands of its troops to the land of the two Holy Mosques [Saudi Arabia] . . . and its support of the oppressive, corrupt and tyrannical regime that is in control. These are the reasons behind the singling out of America as a target.[63]

In its war against America, al Qaeda successfully used suicide bombers in an attack on the USS *Cole* in Yemen on October 12, 2000, and in its attacks on September 11, 2001. During the former incident, seventeen American sailors were killed, thirty-nine were wounded, and a $1 billion warship was crippled. In the latter, thousands of innocent lives were lost and billions of dollars in property was destroyed. "It is a clear victory," bin Laden declared shortly after the event. "Thank Allah America came out of its caves. We hit her the first hit and the next one will hit her with the hands of the believers, the good believers, the strong believers."[64]

Divide and Conquer

Al Qaeda has not confined itself to attacks on America. It also wants to topple Middle Eastern governments that have political ties to the West and that are likely to support democracy, human rights, and the separation of religion and state. Bombings that were carried out in Riyadh, Saudi Arabia, in May and November 2003 were meant to embarrass Saudi leadership, prove its inability to provide security for its people, and ultimately destabilize that government. Bin Laden particularly despises the rulers of Saudi Arabia for allowing America to station troops on its soil.

Much of al Qaeda's strength stems from the fact that it has been able to coordinate with other terrorist groups to achieve its aims. Journalist Peter Bergen describes this phenomenon:

There is al Qaeda, the organization. Most non-specialists [that is, ordinary people] are surprised to learn that al Qaeda has only 200 to 300 members. . . . The second concentric ring spreading out beyond the inner core of al Qaeda consists of perhaps several thousand "holy warriors" trained in the group's Afghan camps. . . . Beyond this circle are tens of thousands of militants who received some kind of basic military training in Afghanistan over the past decade. . . . Finally, untold numbers of Muslims around the world subscribe to bin Laden's . . . worldview that the West is the enemy of Islam. Some of these, too, may be prepared to do violence. [65]

Those Muslims mentioned in the latter group made their anger felt after the fall of Saddam Hussein's regime in 2003. The presence of American soldiers in Iraq sparked resentment, made ordinarily peaceful citizens more sympathetic to terrorist thinking, and led to retaliatory strikes against soldiers. Instability

Stop the Violence

Efrat Gamlieli is a twenty-five-year-old Israeli who lives in a suburb of West Jerusalem. She is training to be an occupational therapist. In "Voices from the Conflict," a special report on the Middle East found on the BBC News Web site, she describes what it is like to live in the midst of violence.

Mostly we are afraid of bombs. If I go to Ben Yehuda market, and I go through there most days, I get through it as fast as I can. It is the most likely place in which I might be exposed to a terrorist attack. . . .

You see many more policemen and soldiers in the city, especially in certain places, but in terms of the day-to-day activities of the people nothing has changed. When I go to the mall, it is like normal. People aren't staying at home. I think it's pretty much life as normal in many ways. . . .

I have known a lot of Arabs in my life. They came to my house, my family treated them as equals, but now even the Israeli Arabs are against us, or were for a while. And this is hard for us because we thought they were part of us. Now we see that they are probably not and this is hard because they live among us. . . .

I hope there will be a peace. But the violence has to stop. . . . Maybe if the violence stops they will go back to talking like at Camp David. We will give up a little and they will give up a little and it could happen that way, otherwise it will be very hard.

produced by the war also motivated some formerly oppressed groups amongst the Kurds and the Iraqi Shiites to use terrorist methods to express their anger and make their points.

The Bloc of the Faithful

Not all terrorist groups in the Middle East are Muslim fundamentalists. A few are Jewish, intent on paving the way for the coming Messiah or punishing those who harm other Jews. One of the most extreme of these groups is Kach ("thus"), founded by Rabbi Meir Kahane in about 1970. Kahane's goal was the restoration of Israel according to the boundaries described in the Bible, as well as the expulsion of non-Jews from Palestine.

Kahane was assassinated in 1990, but members of an offshoot of the original Kach and a new group, Kahane Chai, followed in his footsteps. They organized protests against the Israeli government and harassed and threatened Palestinians in Hebron and the West Bank. In one of its most lethal actions, in November 1992, Kach claimed credit for a grenade attack in the Palestinian butchers' market in Jerusalem. In February 1994, shortly after the signing of the Oslo (Norway) Peace Accords between Israel and the PLO, Kach-supporter Baruch Goldstein opened fire with a machine gun inside a mosque in Hebron. He killed and wounded dozens of people before he was himself killed. Both Kach and Kahane Chai have been outlawed in Israel.

Gush Emunim—literally, "the bloc of the faithful"—is another religious/political activist group that believes that the biblical state of Israel must be restored and the Palestinians expelled. Formed in March 1974, its members not only organized mass protests but began building Jewish settlements on the West Bank and in the Gaza Strip. They also used violence to try to drive Palestinians out of the region. In 1980 car bombings of five West Bank Palestinian mayors resulted the crippling of two. In 1983 the Hebron Islamic College was the target of a machine-gun and grenade attack that killed three Muslim students and wounded thirty-three others.

In 1984 members of Gush Emunim tried to plant bombs on five buses in East Jerusalem. The plot was discovered and blocked by the Israeli security service, Shin Bet. The security service also thwarted a plan to blow up the Dome of the Rock in East Jerusalem in 1984. In the last two decades, the organization has focused its energies on encouraging the growth and influence of Jewish settlements in the occupied areas rather than carrying out overt terrorist activities. Still, it remains open to the use of violence against Palestinians if that will further its aims.

Terrorist Backing

Unlike in Israel, many Middle Eastern governments look the other way while fundamentalist terrorist groups live and operate in their countries. Leaders do this to pacify conservative religious groups who make up a significant portion of the country's population. These groups are inclined to be sympathetic to fundamentalists' beliefs, which are also conservative. Without conservative sup-

money supported radical mosques and schools, paramilitary training camps, the purchase of weapons, and the recruitment of members into terrorist organizations. Their money also helped support groups such as Hamas and al Qaeda. "Islamic activities dominate the leadership of the largest charities," stated a CIA report in 1996. "Even high-ranking members of the collecting or monitoring agencies in Saudi Arabia, Kuwait, and Pakistan—such as the Saudi High Commission—are involved in illicit activities, including support for terrorists."[66]

Some governments sponsor terrorist groups outright in order to gain or maintain power in their country or their region. In such situations, terrorists can have access to even more than money. They may be able to use industrial and military equipment and complexes when they train or lay their plans. They can also easily avoid pursuit within their own borders.

Syria and Libya are two Middle Eastern countries that have sponsored terror in the past. President Hafez al-Assad used terrorists to destroy opposition to his regime, to apply pressure to his enemies in the Arab world, and to further Syria's goals in the Arab-Israeli conflict. His son, Bashar, appears to be following in his father's footsteps. Syria continues to harbor and train terrorist groups, which Bashar refuses to expel, claiming they are breaking no Syrian laws and do not harm Syrian interests. He also denies American charges that he allowed terrorists to cross from Syria into Iraq during the 2003 Iraq War. "There is chaos, there is weapons smuggling and

Terrorists find support in Syria from President Bashar al-Assad.

port, ruling regimes run the risk of being voted out or overthrown.

Saudi Arabia has been a key offender with regard to terrorism, letting unregulated charitable organizations funnel millions of dollars to terrorist groups in the region. The Muslim World League and the International Islamic Relief Organization were two Saudi charities whose

unknown individuals fleeing," he stated. "Of course, the Americans say those are terrorists. Anyone becomes a terrorist for them; maybe they consider any Arab a terrorist."[67]

Muammar Qaddafi of Libya has supported terrorists by providing asylum, weapons, and training camps for their use. For years Qaddafi refused to turn over terrorists who were known to be responsible for the destruction of Pan Am Flight 103 over Lockerbie, Scotland, in 1988. He also sheltered terrorists who carried out a discotheque bombing in Berlin in 1986, and the abduction of a prominent Libyan dissident and human rights activist Mansur Kikhia in 1993. "It is now widely believed that Qadhafi's ruthless security apparatus has executed Mr. Kikhia shortly after his abduction. Qadhafi's . . . policies and his involvement in domestic and international acts of terrorism against innocent civilians . . . have turned Libya into a rogue, pariah state,"[68] reads a letter submitted by the Mansur Kikhia Foundation for Democracy and Human Rights in 2000.

Iran was considered the most active state sponsor of terrorism in 2002. The government's Islamic Revolutionary Guard Corps and its Ministry of Intelligence and Security helped plan and sup-

The Devil Is Dancing

In his book Longitudes and Attitudes, *journalist Thomas L. Friedman reflects on the world after the events of September 11, 2001. In the following excerpt, he points out that tactics used by Palestinian suicide bombers may soon be used with devastating effect in America and other nations if nothing is done to stop them.*

Israelis are terrified. And Palestinians . . . feel a rising sense of empowerment. They feel they finally have a weapon that creates a balance of power with Israel, and maybe, in their fantasies, can defeat Israel. As Ismail Haniya, a Hamas leader, said in the *Washington Post*, Palestinians have Israelis on the run now because they have found their weak spot. Jews, he said, "love life more than any other people, and they prefer not to die." So Palestinian suicide bombers are ideal for dealing with them. . . .

Let us be very clear: Palestinians have adopted suicide bombing as a strategic choice, not out of desperation. This threatens all civilizations because if suicide bombing is allowed to work in Israel, then, like hi-jacking and airplane bombing, it will be copied and will eventually lead to a bomber strapped with a nuclear device threatening entire nations. . . .

The Palestinians are so blinded by their narcissistic [self-important] rage that they have lost sight of the basic truth civilization is built on: the sacredness of every human life, starting with your own. If America, the only reality check left, doesn't use every ounce of energy to halt this madness and call it by its real name, then it will spread. The Devil is dancing in the Middle East, and he's dancing our way.

Iranian Basilj students and hardliners wave pictures of Ayatollah Ali Khamenei and Hezbollah flags in support of Hezbollah.

port terrorist acts throughout the Middle East. It also supported terrorist groups that included Hezbollah and Palestine Islamic Jihad, providing them with funding, training, and weapons. Many al Qaeda members from Afghanistan and elsewhere have found safe haven in Iran as well and are believed to receive protection from the government.

Crackdown

Despite the difficulty of combating terrorism, much progress has been made in recent years. After the attacks of September 11, 2001, a coalition of nations was formed to help topple the fundamentalist Taliban regime that was supporting Osama bin Laden in Afghanistan. Agencies throughout the world began to block terrorists' fund-raising efforts, disrupt their financing networks, and deny them access to international financial systems. Law enforcement and intelligence agencies began to work together to discover suspects and prevent them from striking.

Their efforts were at least somewhat successful. Plots that ranged from shoe bomber Richard Reid's attempt to bring down American Airlines Flight 63 in 2001 to plans by suspected Islamic extremists to set off a car bomb at a military hospital in Hamburg, Germany, in 2004 were discovered and blocked. Governments such as Qaddafi's were convinced to turn over terrorists and dismantle weapons programs. Terrorist rings were broken. Terrorist leaders were captured, killed, or brought to justice.

At the urging of the United States, cooperative governments in the Middle East cracked down on terrorists in order to save innocent lives. Saudi Arabia thwarted attacks, arrested hundreds of suspects, and captured large amounts of explosives and weapons. Israel increased its retaliatory attacks against suicide bombers by bombing homes of suspected terrorists and killing militant leaders like Salah Shehada, head of Palestinian Hamas, and Mekled Hameid, a top Islamic Jihad commander. These two terrorists were responsible for hundreds of attacks and bombings against Israeli civilians in recent years.

Those who are committed to rooting out terrorism know the path will not be easy. The causes of such violence are complex and deep-rooted. Large numbers of people must participate if progress is to be made. As President Bush emphasized in August 2003, "In continued acts of murder and destruction, terrorists are testing our will, hoping we will weaken and withdraw. Yet across the world, they are finding that our will cannot be shaken. Whatever the hardships, we will persevere."[69]

CHAPTER 7

Prospects and Possibilities

There is no easy way to end conflict in the Middle East. Centuries of discord over religion, regimes, and resources have left deep-seated bitterness and resentment that may never fade away. Poverty, repression, and unresponsive leaders have, for some, made violence the only way to bring about change. And even those who want peace in their day-to-day lives have trouble putting aside their long-standing doubt and distrust. "We're afraid of each other," stated Rabbi Steven Riskin. "That's the tragedy of this situation."[70]

Despite the hostility, there are those who believe the violence can be curbed, if not eliminated. "I've been interested for a long time in improving relations between Jews and Arabs," states Israeli Limor Gabriel, a member of a group called Interns for Peace. The organization works in Israel, Palestine, Gaza/West Bank, Jordan, and Egypt to promote community interaction that will lead to peace. "My parents think that what Interns for Peace is doing can't work. But I believe it's possible for Arabs and Jews to live in peace. You have to think that, you have to believe that. When the situation is as bad as it is now, you have to keep hope."[71]

The Hopeful

Interns for Peace is only one group that believes that conditions can improve in the Middle East. There are others as well. The Families Forum, formed in 1994, is an organization of parents—both Jewish and Palestinian—who have lost children to terrorist acts. They push for peace and reconciliation, and work to prevent grief from deepening hostility between peoples. The Middle East Activist Group, formed in May 2002 by people of differing religious, ethnic, and political backgrounds, works to build cross-cultural friendships as well as eliminate fear and ignorance that leads to conflict. The Middle East Peace Dialogue Network, founded in the late 1990s, supports better communication between Israelis and Palestinians and promotes an exchange of ideas through shared economic development, the arts, workshops, and lectures.

Those who work for peace point out that there are practical benefits to laying aside hostilities and negotiating compromises. Basically, peace is good for business; trade agreements between formerly hostile neighbors could strengthen economies. And money that would ordinarily go toward fighting a war or supporting a strong military could be channeled into more constructive enterprises.

Lebanon is one example of a country that is just beginning to enjoy the benefits of peace again. Most of the militias have been weakened or disbanded, and under the Taif Accord—a blueprint for national reconciliation—the political system has been made more equitable by giving Muslims a greater say in the political process.

In turn, transportation, power, telecommunications, and other systems are being reestablished. Ordinary Lebanese are working hard to get their lives back to normal. Homes and buildings have been rebuilt. Shop owners operate businesses that range from fruit stands to Persian carpet salons out of the basements of bombed-out buildings. "The entrepreneurial spirit of the Lebanese people is their greatest asset," remarks Ghassan Jamous, a representative of the U.S. Agency for International Development in Lebanon. "The Lebanese know how to work and they refuse to give up."[72]

Still, problems remain. The nation is faced with debt. Syrian forces still oc-

The Meaning of Peace

In his book A Concise History of the Middle East, *author Arthur Goldschmidt Jr. asks the question "What do we mean by 'peace'?" He explores the meaning of that question for people in the Middle East and suggests that, even over such a small matter, there is the potential for disagreement.*

When addressing the question of peace with Israel, some Arabs say that they will accept *salam* but not *sulh*. What is the difference? Both words mean "peace," but in the modern usage *salam* carries the connotation of a temporary cessation of hostilities. The word *sulh* means "reconciliation." Arabs who make this distinction may envisage an armistice with Israel, a respite from hostilities during which they can regain their political and economic strength, but not a true reconciliation with the Jewish state. As this distinction naturally arouses the fears of Israel and its supporters, stressing it hardly seems likely to lead to peace.

cupy the country. Hezbollah continues to operate in the south. People are hopeful, however. In 2004 Lebanese prime minister Rafik Hariri emphasized that even greater efforts are necessary to finish what has been started in recent years: "We have to see the problems all together and try to solve them all together because living together is essential for the Lebanese people. We cannot do it otherwise."[73]

Brokering Peace

Motivated by humanitarian as well as political and economic reasons, peacemakers have made repeated efforts over the years to bring an end to hostilities in the region. The Israelis and their enemies are of particular concern, and the United States has been the prime negotiator in many of those conflicts. One of the first U.S. envoys to focus on Middle Eastern problems was Secretary of State William Rogers, who, in 1969, called for peace based on Israel's returning land it had won in 1967. The Rogers Plan fell apart after all sides refused to comply with its terms.

A 1974 peace effort led by U.S. secretary of state Henry Kissinger was more successful. Kissinger traveled to the Middle East after the 1973 Yom Kippur War. He was able to cool hot tempers and negotiate a temporary cease-fire between Israeli, Egyptian, and Syrian forces. In 1975 his continued diplomacy paid off as Egypt and Israel signed the Sinai Agreement. It stated in part:

The Government of the Arab Republic of Egypt and the Government of Israel have agreed that the conflict between them in the Middle East shall not be resolved by military force but by peaceful means. . . . The Parties hereby undertake not to resort to the threat or use of force or military blockade against each other. The Parties shall continue scrupulously to observe the ceasefire on land, sea and air and to refrain from all military or paramilitary actions against each other.[74]

In 1977 President Jimmy Carter took another step closer to peace when he presided over the Camp David Accords. During this series of meetings that took place in Camp David, Maryland, Egypt's President Anwar Sadat and Israel's Prime Minister Menachem Begin put their differences behind them and made major concessions that marked the formal end of hostilities between the two nations. Carter was recognized for his peacemaker ability, a gift he would use many times in later years.

Peace between Egypt and Israel was established, but the problem of Israel and the Palestinians remained. Both sides remained unwilling to acknowledge the legitimacy of the other, so all discussions had to be carried out through middlemen. This was a hindrance to progress. In 1993, however, the Norwegian government was able to bring together Israeli prime minister Yitzhak Rabin and PLO chairman Yasir Arafat for secret meetings in Oslo, Norway. There, they successfully hammered out the Oslo Accords, which were signed on August 20, 1993. In the accords, both parties agreed

Israeli prime minister Ehud Barak (left), American president Bill Clinton, and Palestinian leader Yasir Arafat meet at Camp David in 2000.

to the withdrawal of Israeli forces from the Gaza Strip and the West Bank and to Palestinians' right to self-government in those areas. Difficult issues such as Jerusalem, refugees, settlements, security, and borders remained to be settled at a future date. The two enemies formally shook hands at a public ceremony in Washington, D.C., on September 13, 1993, with President Bill Clinton presiding.

Clinton met with Arafat and Israeli prime minister Ehud Barak to continue the Oslo negotiations in the year 2000. The Camp David 2000 Summit, as it was known, ended in failure, however. Attacks on Israelis by Palestinians and the growing number of Jewish settlements on the West Bank left both sides unwilling to compromise or grant concessions. Diplomatic relations fell apart.

"Road Map Toward Peace"

The latest attempt at peace came in 2003, when President George W. Bush declared his intention to establish a road map for peace for Israel and the Palestinians. With the backing of the United States, the European Union, the United Nations, and Russia, a three-part plan was suggested in which terrorism and violence would cease and an independent, democratic, and viable Palestinian state would be established. Bush observed on March 14, 2003:

> The time has come to move beyond entrenched positions and to take concrete actions to achieve peace.

America is committed, and I am personally committed, to implementing our road map toward peace. Our efforts are guided by clear principles: We believe that all people in the Middle East—Arab and Israeli alike—deserve to live in dignity, under free and honest governments. We believe that people who live in freedom are more likely to reject bitterness, blind hatred and terror; and are far more likely to turn their energy toward reconciliation, reform and development. [75]

Barely a week after Israeli prime minister Ariel Sharon and Palestinian prime

No Magic Answer

Since becoming president in 1977, Jimmy Carter has pursued peace in the Middle East. In an excerpt from the final chapter of his book The Blood of Abraham, *he looks to the future and shares his hopes for the region.*

There is no magic answer to the Middle East puzzle, and it is unrealistic to address the extremely complex issues and conflicting points of view with any marked degree of optimism. . . . At the same time, it is impossible to abandon the search for peace in spite of the almost insurmountable obstacles.

The questions to be considered are almost endless: What possibilities does the future hold? What are the prime requisites for peace? Can there be a relatively stable peace that merely perpetuates the present circumstances and trends? Will those who are aggrieved be content to wait quietly for a doubtful peace settlement in the distant future? Must the situation steadily deteriorate until another crisis causes the interested parties to act? . . . Most chilling of all, could the present differences lead to the use of nuclear weapons? . . .

I have spent a substantial portion of my public life dealing with these questions; more recently, I have spoken to literally hundreds of people in order to get the broadest and most balanced view possible. I have always been sustained in times of greatest discouragement by the conviction that the people in the region . . . want the peace efforts to succeed.

minister Mahmoud Abbas agreed to the road map on June 4, 2003, Palestinian militants killed four Israeli soldiers. Other violent incidents on the part of the Palestinians followed, drawing reprisals from Israel. Hopes for a peaceful settlement between Israelis and Palestinians faded again.

Bringing Peace to Israel

The Israeli-Palestinian conflict is perhaps the most difficult challenge to peace in the Middle East today. Before a solution can be found, both sides will have to come to terms with the fact that compromise is necessary; that two sovereign states will have to be carved out of disputed land; and that each state will be permanent, the national home of its people.

Progress will be more likely if both sides adopt a vision of what they can achieve and what they will gain if they compromise. For Palestinians, that will be the opportunity to improve their economic and social circumstances. For Israelis, it will be the opportunity to live without fear. Adopting that new vision will involve seeing things from a different angle, understanding that peace and prosperity is better than war, and believing that both sides can somehow live side by side without killing each other.

It will be difficult to achieve. The notion of giving up land is as offensive to Israelis as recognizing the statehood of Israel is to Palestinians. Innumerable details relating to security, borders, settlements, and other issues will also need creativity and patience to resolve. Thus, the peace solution will likely have to be brokered by an outside party. Finally, everyone will have to face the fact that, even if compromise is reached, both sides will remain deeply dissatisfied. Thomas Friedman suggests a practical response:

America, in effect, has to say to both Israelis and Palestinians, "You are two people with nothing in common— not language, not history, not culture, and not religion. I am not asking you to love each other. I don't expect you to love each other. The sooner you live apart, the better off you will both be. But the only way you can hope to live apart and at peace is by first coming together to produce a settlement that guarantees Israelis their security and Palestinians their right to self-determination in the West Bank and Gaza Strip. Nothing short of that will ever bring peace."[76]

"We Shall Not Be Deterred"

A second challenge to peace in the Middle East is bringing terrorism under control. Terrorists are cunning, determined, and unnoticeable until they strike. Most will use any means to further their cause. They enjoy financial and moral support from many who believe in violence but are not comfortable carrying out violent acts themselves. And given the right circumstances—a continuing U.S. presence in Iraq or anger with the Saudi government—even peaceful individuals might grow angry enough to join the activists, thus adding to their numbers.

Perhaps the best way to undermine terrorism is to establish moderate, pro-

Palestinian demonstrators clash with Israeli soldiers in the West Bank. The Israeli-Palestinian conflict remains the most difficult challenge to peace in the Middle East today.

gressive Middle Eastern governments headed by men and women who are capable of addressing inequalities and injustices within their countries. When the poor and powerless are given a chance to be heard, and to enjoy the benefits of a free and prosperous society, they will be less likely to turn to violence to achieve their aims. As Vice President Dick Cheney observed in January 2004, "Democracies do not breed the anger and the radicalism that drag down whole societies or export violence. Terrorists do not find fertile recruiting grounds in societies where young people have the right to decide their own destinies and choose their own leaders."[77]

Without the emergence of responsible governments in the Middle East, dedicated and conscientious leaders from around the world will be needed to do what they can to curb terrorism. One example of such a leader is UN secretary-general Kofi Annan, who in 2003 promised to press ahead with efforts to rebuild Iraq, despite devastating attacks by rebels and terrorists there. "We will carry on our work," he said. "We shall not be deterred. We are going to keep at it until we succeed."[78]

Peace activists demonstrate in Israel. After decades of warfare, many believe that compromise is the only means of bringing peace to the Israeli-Palestinian conflict.

If enough people are convinced that moderation and cooperation are preferable alternatives to extremism and intolerance, peace can become a reality in the Middle East. Leaders and ordinary people alike will have to be willing to put their hatreds and their differences behind them, however. When that will be remains unclear.

American University psychologist Richard Day posed a telling question in 1984, when he was living in Beirut and watching the devastation the war was causing. "When will there be peace in Lebanon?" he asked himself. His answer was simple: "When the Lebanese start to love their children more than they hate each other."[79] The same answer holds true for all the people in the Middle East. Peace will be a struggle, but when enough peaceable men, women, and children work, dream, and persist long enough, it can be achieved.

NOTES

Introduction: Region in Turmoil

1. Arthur Goldschmidt Jr., *A Concise History of the Middle East*. Boulder, CO: Westview Press, 1979, p. 373.
2. Quoted in U.S. Department of State's Office of International Information Programs, "Burns Asks Senate for $200 Million for Middle East Partnership Initiative," March 26, 2003. http://usinfo.state.gov/regional/nea/iraq/text2003/0326burns.htm.
3. Irving Kett, "Strategic Challenges in the Middle East," Freeman Center for Strategic Studies, May 2001. www.freeman.org/m_online/may01/kett.htm.
4. Quoted in Council on Foreign Relations, "Causes of 9/11: World Poverty?" 2004. www.terrorismanswers.com/causes/poverty.html.

Chapter 1: Holy Ground: Religion in the Middle East

5. John and Carol Loeffler, "The Middle East Word War," *Newswith Views.com*, April 11, 2002. www.newswithviews.com/loeffler/loeffler3.htm.
6. Ehud Barak, "Address by Prime Minister Ehud Barak at Opening Ceremony of Holocaust Martyrs' and Heroes' Remembrance Day," Israel Ministry of Foreign Affairs, May 1, 2000. www.mfa.gov.il/mfa/go.asp?MFAH0 h9j0.
7. Quoted in PBS, "What Muslims Believe," 2002. www.pbs.org/wgbh/pages/frontline/shows/muslims/etc/what.html.
8. Jonathan Marcus, "Secularism vs. Orthodox Judaism," *BBC News*, April 22, 1998. http://news.bbc.co.uk/2/hi/events/israel_at_50/israel_today/81033.stm.
9. Quoted in *Charity Wire*, "Common Ground for Christians, Muslims Crucial but Elusive," May 6, 2000. www.charitywire.com/charity96/01457.html.

Chapter 2: Outside Forces

10. Bernard Lewis, *What Went Wrong? Western Impact and Middle Eastern Response*. New York: Oxford University Press, 2002, p. 153.
11. Goldschmidt, *A Concise History of the Middle East*, p. 164.
12. Goldschmidt, *A Concise History of the Middle East*, p. 195.

13. William L. Cleveland, *A History of the Modern Middle East*. Boulder, CO: Westview Press, 1994, p. 191.

14. Quoted in National Geographic Society, ed., *Cradle and Crucible: History and Faith in the Middle East*. Washington, DC: National Geographic Society, 2002, p. 131.

15. Thomas L. Friedman, *From Beirut to Jerusalem*. New York: Farrar, Straus, and Giroux, 1989, p. 98.

16. Jimmy Carter, "State of the Union Address," Jimmy Carter Library and Museum, January 21, 1980. www.jimmycarterlibrary.org/documents/speeches/su80jec.phtml.

17. Quoted in Tarik Kafala, "Analysis: Region Opposes Attack on Iraq," *BBC News*, March 18, 2002. http://news.bbc.co.uk/2/hi/middle_east/1879066.stm.

18. Patrick J. Buchanan, "Wrong War in the Wrong Place," *American Cause*, September 15, 2003. www.theamericancause.org/patwrongwarinthewrongplaceprint.htm.

19. Quoted in Friedman, *From Beirut to Jerusalem*, p. 210.

20. Quoted in National Geographic Society, *Cradle and Crucible*, p. 130.

Chapter 3: Yours or Mine?

21. James J. Puplava, "Riders on the Storm," *Financial Sense Online*, August 16, 2001. www.financialsense.com/series2/riders/shift.htm.

22. Maurice Strong, "Peace, Security, and Sustainability," Simon Fraser University, January 16, 2003. www.sfu.ca/blaneyaward/strong_speech2003.htm.

23. Yedidya Atlas, "Israel's Water Basics," Freeman Center for Strategic Studies, November 1999. www.freeman.org/m_online/nov99/atlas.htm.

24. Quoted in Adel Darwish, "When the Tap Was Turned Off," *Mideast News*, 2003. www.mideastnews.com/Turkey_Syria.htm.

25. Cleveland, *A History of the Modern Middle East*, p. 390.

26. Quoted in Saudi Arabian Information Source, "Kingdom and Qatar Borders," March 21, 2001. www.saudinf.com/main/y2289.htm.

27. Quoted in Middle East Media Research Institute, "Arafat on the 33rd Anniversary of the Death of Egyptian President Abd al-Nasser," September 28, 2003. www.memri.de/uebersetzungen_analysen/laender/palaestinensische_a_gebiete/pa_arafat_nasser_02_10_03.pdf.

28. Quoted in Daniel Pipes, "Greater Syria," Cedarland, 2004. www.geocities.com/CapitolHill/Parliament/2587/syria.html.

29. Quoted in Pipes, "Greater Syria."

30. Quoted in American-Israeli Cooperative Enterprise, "Syria's Role in Lebanon," 2004. www.us-israel.org/jsource/History/Syria's_role_in_Leb.htm.

Chapter 4: The Struggle to Rule

31. Quoted in Congressional Quarterly, *The Middle East*. Washington, DC:

Congressional Quarterly Press, 2000, p. 336.

32. Quoted in Congressional Quarterly, *The Middle East*, p. 230.

33. Quoted in National Geographic Society, *Cradle and Crucible*, pp. 193–94.

34. Quoted in Tim Sullivan, "Women See Few Gains in Kuwait 'Democracy,'" Arab Regional Resource Center on Violence Against Women, December 10, 2002. www.amanjordan. org/english/daily_news/wmview.php? ArtID=527.

35. Quoted in Seyyed Rasuli, "The Pyramid of Skulls: How Saddam Hussein Came to Power," *International Review*, February 20, 2003. www.geocities. com/Paris/Rue/4637/terr37a.html.

36. Quoted in *BBC News*, "Mass Graves 'Hold 300,000 Iraqis,'" November 8, 2003. http://news.bbc.co.uk/2/hi/ middle_east/3253783.stm.

37. Milton Viorst, "Ayatollah Ruhollah Khomeini," *Time*, April 13, 1998. www.time.com/time/time100/leaders/ profile/khomeini.html.

38. Quoted in Howard Schneider, "Iran's Voters Put Pragmatism Above Philosophy," *Washington Post* Foreign Service. February 25, 2000. www. library.cornell.edu/colldev/mideast/ irnprag.htm.

39. Judith Miller, *God Has Ninety-nine Names: Reporting from a Militant Middle East*. New York: Simon & Schuster, 1996, p. 341.

40. Quoted in CNN, "'Soldier for Peace,' Rabin Buried," November 6, 1995.
www.cnn.com/WORLD/9511/rabin/ funeral/wrap/index.html.

41. Quoted in Sarah McCrum, "Peace Has to Be Between People, You Can't Buy It," *OneWorld.net*, 1993. www.one world.org/peacequest/stories/ilkids. html.

Chapter 5: Clash over Palestine

42. Jimmy Carter, *The Blood of Abraham*. Boston: Houghton Mifflin, 1985, p. 113.

43. Quoted in *World Zionist Organization*, "The Zionist Exposition," 2003. www.wzo.org.il/home/move ment/herzl.htm.

44. Israel Ministry of Foreign Affairs, "The Balfour Declaration," November 2, 1917. www.mfa.gov.il/mfa/ home.asp.

45. Quoted in Edward W. Said, *The Question of Palestine*. New York: Vintage Books, 1992, p. 14.

46. Avalon Project at Yale Law School, "Declaration of Israel's Independence 1948," May 14, 1948. www.yale.edu/ lawweb/avalon/mideast/israel. htm.

47. Quoted in Mitchell Bard, "The 1948 War," American-Israeli Cooperative Enterprise, 2004. www.us-israel.org/ jsource/History/1948_War.html.

48. Quoted in Jewish Agency for Israel, "Israel and Zionism," 2004. www.jafi. org.il/education/100/maps/pos.html.

49. Goldschmidt, *A Concise History of the Middle East*, p. 264.

50. Quoted in Friedman, *From Beirut to Jerusalem*. p. 378.

51. Quoted in *Salt Lake Tribune*, "Suicide Bombing Elicits Call for Action," October 5, 2003. www.sltrib.com/2003/Oct/10052003/nation_w/988 25.asp.

52. Israel Ministry of Foreign Affairs, "U.N. Security Council Resolution 242," November 22, 1967. www.mfa.gov.il/mfa/go.asp?MFAH00p40.

53. Quoted in Ed O'Loughlin, "Running the Snipers' Gauntlet in the West Bank's Frontier of Hate," *Sydney Morning Herald*, June 28, 2003. www.smh.com.au/articles/2003/06/27/1056683906559.html.

54. Quoted in *BBC News*, "Voices from the Conflict," 2002. http://news.bbc.co.uk/hi/english/static/in_depth/middle_east/2000/voices_of_conflict/shimlawi.stm.

55. Quoted in *BBC News*, "Arafat Denounces 'Racist' Fence," June 17, 2002. http://news.bbc.co.uk/2/hi/middle_east/2049812.stm.

56. Meir Shlomo, "The Arafat Fence," *Providence Journal*, December 9, 2003. www.israelemb.org/boston/fence.html#newman.

57. Colin L. Powell, "United States Position on Terrorists and Peace in the Middle East," November 19, 2001. Embassy of the Hashimite kingdom of Jordan. www.jordanembassyus.org/speech_powell111901.htm.

Chapter 6: Terrorism and the Middle East

58. Friedman, *From Beirut to Jerusalem*, p. 507.

59. Thomas Friedman, "Trust, Shame at Core of War on Terror," *Tacoma News Tribune*, January 9, 2004. www.tribnet.com/opinion/columnists/thomas_friedman/story/4595888 p-4565583c.html.

60. Quoted in Bruce Murray, "Making Sense of Fundamentalists," Foundation for American Communications, 2004. www.facsnet.org/issues/faith/antoun.php3.

61. Abdulaziz Sachedina, "From Defensive to Offensive Warfare: The Use and Abuse of Jihad in the Muslim World," Organization for Islamic Learning, 2002. www.people.virginia.edu/~aas/article/article8.htm.

62. Quoted in *Sydney Morning Herald*, "Al-Aqsa Martyrs Brigades Reject Truce," November 20, 2003. www.smh.com.au/articles/2003/11/19/1069027186322.html.

63. Quoted in *PBS Frontline*, "Who Is Osama Bin Laden?" May 1998. www.jihadunspun.net/BinLadens Network/interviews/pbsfrontline 05-1998.cfm.

64. Embassy of the USA, "Transcript: Videotape of Usama Bin Laden Discussing September 11 Attacks," December 13, 2001. www.usembassy.sk/cis/cisen020.html.

65. Peter Bergen, "What Is Al Qaeda?" 2003. www.peterbergen.com/clients/PeterBergen/pbergen.nsf/Web00002 Show?OpenForm&ParentUNID= 44D09381A774568285256CBF006 077D1.

66. Quoted in David E. Kaplan, "The Saudi Connection," *U.S. News & World Report*, December 15, 2003, pp. 25–26.

67. Quoted in Neil MacFarquar, "Syrian Leader Says Israel Aims to Stir Region," *New York Times*, October 8, 2003, p. A16.

68. Quoted in *LibyaNet.com*, "Protest Against the Flagrant Abuse of Human Rights by Mu'ammar al-Qadhafi's Regime," 2001.www.libya net.com/v09aug1c.htm.

69. George W. Bush, "President's Radio Address," August 23, 2003. The White House, www.whitehouse. gov/news/releases/2003/08/2003 0823.html.

Chapter 7: Prospects and Possibilities

70. Quoted in John and Janet Wallach, *Still Small Voices*. New York: Harcourt Brace Jovanovich, 1989, p. 205.

71. Quoted in Katie Monagle, "Growing Up in a Land of Conflict," *Scholastic Update*, October 4, 1991, p. 15.

72. Quoted in Karen Homer, "Beirut: Rising from the Rubble," World Vision, October 1996. www.worldvision.org/ worldvision/mag.nsf/0/5e7e94ec2 cc7255488256775007672ee?Open Document.

73. Quoted in Mohammed Alkhereiji, "Hariri Explains How to Rebuild an Economy," *Arab News*, January 19, 2004. www.arabnews.com/?page=1 &section=0&article=38245&d=19 &m=1&y=2004&pix=kingdom.jpg &category=Kingdom.

74. Chaim Herzog Center for Middle East Studies and Diplomacy, "The Sinai Agreement," September 4, 1975. www.bgu.ac.il/chcenter/05 historical_documents/sinai_ agreement.htm.

75. George W. Bush, "President Discusses Roadmap for Peace in the Middle East," March 14, 2003. The White House, www.whitehouse.gov/news/ releases/2003/03/20030314-4.html.

76. Friedman, *From Beirut to Jerusalem*, p. 500.

77. Quoted in Jim Garamone, "Cheney Says Democracies Must Confront Terror Together," U.S. Department of Defense, January 26, 2004. www. defenselink.mil/news/Jan2004/n0126 2004_200401262.html.

78. Quoted in CNN, "Pentagon: Possible al Qaeda Link in Baghdad Blast," August 20, 2003. www.cnn. com/2003/WORLD/meast/08/20/sp rj.irq.main.

79. Quoted in Friedman, *From Beirut to Jerusalem*, p. 230.

FOR FURTHER READING

Books

David J. Abodaher, *Youth in the Middle East: Voices of Despair*. New York: Franklin Watts, 1990. Interviews with young people in the Middle East illustrate the political strife there and how it has affected their lives.

Michael Kort, *The Handbook of the Middle East*. Brookfield, CT: Twenty-First Century Books, 2002. Examines the past, present, and future of countries in the Middle East.

Cathryn J. Long, *The Middle East in Search of Peace*. Brookfield, CT: Millbrook Press, 1994. Covers conflict and peace efforts in the Middle East up to 1994. Good photos.

Mary E. Williams, ed., *The Middle East: Opposing Viewpoints*. San Diego: Greenhaven Press, 2000. This book deals with questions such as "Why is the Middle East a conflict area?" "How does religion affect the Middle East?" "What role should the United States play in the Middle East?" and "How could peace be advanced in the Middle East?"

Web Sites

Middle East Activist (www.meactivist. org). Information about the organization that attempts to resolve conflict in the Middle East by promoting education and cross-cultural friendship. The site offers publications, programs, and other ways to learn about and get involved in the issues.

Middle East Peace Dialogue Network (www.mpdn.org). The network works for peace in the Middle East. The site gives information on a variety of topics, including groups such as the Hapoel Youth Program, Interns for Peace, and Seeds of Peace, all of which work to promote greater understanding between Israeli and Palestinian young people.

WORKS CONSULTED

Books

Jimmy Carter, *The Blood of Abraham*. Boston: Houghton Mifflin, 1985. The thirty-ninth president of the United States gives an overview of political, religious, and ethnic conflicts in the Middle East.

William L. Cleveland, *A History of the Modern Middle East*. Boulder, CO: Westview Press, 1994. An analysis of the last two centuries of Middle Eastern history.

Congressional Quarterly, *The Middle East*. Washington, DC: Congressional Quarterly Press, 2000. This work contains profiles of Middle Eastern countries and leaders, a chronology of major events, texts of major documents, and other valuable information.

Thomas L. Friedman, *From Beirut to Jerusalem*. New York: Farrar, Straus, and Giroux, 1989. Friedman, a five-time Pulitzer Prize–winning author, gives a fascinating firsthand look at life in Beirut and Jerusalem in the 1980s.

———, *Longitudes and Attitudes: Exploring the World After September 11*. New York: Farrar, Straus and Giroux, 2002. An excellent collection of commentaries on the Middle East and the world.

Deborah J. Gerner, ed., *Understanding the Contemporary Middle East*. Boulder, CO: Lynne Rienner, 2000. More than a dozen scholars contribute chapters on the Middle East, discussing issues such as international relationships, population growth, the role of women, and future trends.

Arthur Goldschmidt Jr., *A Concise History of the Middle East*. Boulder, CO: Westview Press, 1979. A fairly lively account of the history of the Middle East that is well organized and easy to follow.

Bernard Lewis, *The Middle East: A Brief History of the Last 2,000 Years*. New York: Scribner's, 1995. Lewis, a foremost authority on the Middle East, provides a balanced, penetrating, and comprehensive look at history, economics, law, religion, culture, and other topics.

———, *What Went Wrong? Western Impact and Middle Eastern Response*. New York: Oxford University Press, 2002.

Lewis examines the reaction of the Islamic world as it changed from a foremost power in early times to being dominated by the West in the twentieth century.

Judith Miller, *God Has Ninety-nine Names: Reporting from a Militant Middle East*. New York: Simon & Schuster, 1996. Miller, a correspondent for the *New York Times*, takes a first-hand look at militant Islamic movements in several Middle Eastern countries.

National Geographic Society, ed., *Cradle and Crucible: History and Faith in the Middle East*. Washington, DC: National Geographic Society, 2002. Leading writers in their fields examine reasons why the Middle East is such a tumultuous region. Includes informative overviews of Judaism, Islam, and Christianity.

Ritchie Ovendale, *The Middle East Since 1914*. New York: Longman, 1992. A reference volume that includes chronologies of topics such as terrorism, the birth of Israel, and the significance of oil. Also includes short biographies on leading statesmen, a section on religion, a glossary of terms, and an annotated bibliography.

Edward W. Said, *The Question of Palestine*. New York: Vintage Books, 1992. Slightly dated but still gives valuable background information on decades of clashes between Israelis and Palestinians.

John and Janet Wallach, *Still Small Voices*. New York: Harcourt Brace Jovanovich, 1989. A profile of twelve men and women who live in the West Bank and Gaza Strip.

Periodicals

Dexter Filkins, "U.S. Says Files Seek Qaeda Aid in Iraq Conflict," *New York Times*, February 9, 2004. The article focuses on a document regarding terror in Iraq that was allegedly written by an al Qaeda operative in mid-January 2004.

Peter H. Gleick, Peter Yolles, and Haleh Hatami, "Water, War, and Peace in the Middle East," *Environment*, April 1994. The authors discuss the history of water conflicts, which have escalated in modern times.

David E. Kaplan, "The Saudi Connection," *U.S. News & World Report*, December 15, 2003. Kaplan reveals Saudi Arabia's financial involvement in global terrorism.

Neil MacFarquar, "Syrian Leader Says Israel Aims to Stir Region," *New York Times*, October 8, 2003. President Bashar al-Assad of Syria presents his views on Israel and its motives in the region.

Katie Monagle, "Growing Up in a Land of Conflict," *Scholastic Update*, October 4, 1991. The author interviewed several Israeli and Palestinian young people; she presents their views on war and peace.

Internet Sources

ABC News, "Profile of Yasser Arafat, President of Palestinian Council," 2004. http://abcnews.go.com/sections/

world/WorldNewsTonight/profile_
arafat.html.

Mohammed Alkhereiji, "Hariri Explains How to Rebuild an Economy," *Arab News*, January 19, 2004. www.arabnews.com/?page=1&section=0&article=38245&d=19&m=1&y=2004&pix=kingdom.jpg&category=Kingdom.

American-Israeli Cooperative Enterprise, "Syria's Role in Lebanon," 2004. www.us-israel.org/jsource/History/Syria's_role_in_Leb.html.

Arab Net, "Nasserist Rule," 2002. www.arab.net/egypt/et_nasser.htm.

Yedidya Atlas, "Israel's Water Basics," Freeman Center for Strategic Studies, November 1999. www.freeman.org/m_online/nov99/atlas.htm.

Israel Ministry of Foreign Affairs, "The Balfour Declaration," November 2, 1917, Israel Ministry of Foreign Affairs. ww.mfa.gov.il/mfa/home.asp.

Ehud Barak, "Address by Prime Minister Ehud Barak at Opening Ceremony of Holocaust Martyrs' and Heroes' Remembrance Day," Israel Ministry of Foreign Affairs, May 1, 2000. www.mfa.gov.il/mfa/go.asp?MFAH0h9j0.

Mitchell Bard, "The 1948 War," American-Israeli Cooperative Enterprise, 2004. www.us-israel.org/jsource/History/1948_War.html.

BBC News, "Arafat Denounces 'Racist' Fence," June 17, 2002. http://news.bbc.co.uk/2/hi/middle_east/2049812.stm.

———, "Mass Graves 'Hold 300,000 Iraqis,'" November 8, 2003. http://news.bbc.co.uk/2/hi/middle_east/3253783.stm.

———, "Voices from the Conflict," 2002. http://news.bbc.co.uk/hi/english/static/in_depth/middle_east/2000/voices_of_conflict/shimlawi.stm.

Peter Bergen, "What Is Al Qaeda?" 2003. www.peterbergen.com/clients/PeterBergen/pbergen.nsf/Web00002Show?OpenForm&ParentUNID=44D09381A774568285256CBF006077D1.

Ilan Berman and Paul Michael Wihbey, "The New Water Politics of the Middle East," Institute for Advanced Strategic and Political Studies, 1999. www.israeleconomy.org/strategic/water.htm.

Patrick J. Buchanan, "Wrong War in the Wrong Place," *American Cause*, September 15, 2003. www.theamericancause.org/patwrongwarinthewrongplaceprint.htm.

George W. Bush, "President Discusses Roadmap for Peace in the Middle East," March 14, 2003. The White House, www.whitehouse.gov/news/releases/2003/03/20030314-4.html.

———, "President's Radio Address," August 23, 2003. The White House, www.whitehouse.gov/news/releases/2003/08/20030823.html.

Jimmy Carter, "State of the Union Address," Jimmy Carter Library and Museum, January 21, 1980. www.jimmycarterlibrary.org/documents/speeches/su80jec.phtml.

Charity Wire, "Common Ground for Christians, Muslims Crucial but Elusive," May 6, 2000. www.charitywire.com/charity96/01457.html.

CNN, "Pentagon: Possible al Qaeda Link in Baghdad Blast," August 20, 2003. www.cnn.com/2003/WORLD/meast/08/20/sprj.irq.main.

———, "'Soldier for Peace,' Rabin Buried," November 6, 1995. www.cnn.com/WORLD/9511/rabin/funeral/wrap/index.html.

Council on Foreign Relation, "Causes of 9/11: World Poverty?" 2004. www.terrorismanswers.com/causes/poverty.html.

Adel Darwish, "When the Tap Was Turned Off," *Mideast News*, 2003. www.mideastnews.com/Turkey_Syria.htm.

Avalon Project at Yale Law School. "Declaration of Israel's Independence 1948," May 14, 1948. www.yale.edu/lawweb/avalon/mideast/israel.htm.

Embassy of the USA, "Transcript: Videotape of Usama Bin Laden Discussing September 11 Attacks," December 13, 2001. www.usembassy.sk/cis/cisen020.html.

Thomas Friedman, "Trust, Shame at Core of War on Terror," *Tacoma News Tribune*, January 9, 2004. www.tribnet.com/opinion/columnists/thomas_friedman/story/4595888p-4565583c.html.

Jim Garamone, "Cheney Says Democracies Must Confront Terror Together," U.S. Department of Defense, January 26, 2004. www.defenselink.mil/news/Jan2004/n01262004_20040 1262.html.

Karen Homer, "Beirut: Rising from the Rubble," World Vision, October 1996. www.worldvision.org/worldvision/mag.nsf/0/5e7e94ec2cc7255488256775007672ee?OpenDocument.

R. Stephen Humphreys, *Between Memory and Desire: The Middle East in a Troubled Age*. Berkeley and Los Angeles: University of California Press, 1999. www.ucpress.edu/books/pages/8188/8188.ch01.html.

Ahmed Janabi, "The Arab League: Fifty-nine Years On," Aljazeera.net, March 22, 2004. http://english.aljazeera.net.

Jewish Agency for Israel, "Israel and Zionism," 2004. www.jafi.org.il/education/100/maps/pos.html.

Tarik Kafala, "Analysis: Region Opposes Attack on Iraq," *BBC News*, March 18, 2002. http://news.bbc.co.uk/2/hi/middle_east/1879066.stm.

Azam Kamguian, "Islam and Women's Rights," Institute for the Secularisation of Islamic Society, 2004. www.secularislam.org/women/womislam.htm.

Irving Kett, "Strategic Challenges in the Middle East," Freeman Center for Strategic Studies, May 2001. www.freeman.org/m_online/may01/kett.htm.

LibyaNet.com, "Protest Against the Flagrant Abuse of Human Rights by Mu'ammar al-Qadhafi's Regime," 2001. www.libyanet.com/v09aug1c.htm.

John and Carol Loeffler, "The Middle East Word War," *NewswithViews.com*, April 11, 2002. www.newswithviews.com/loeffler/loeffler3.htm.

Jonathan Marcus, "Secularism vs. Orthodox Judaism," *BBC News*, April 22, 1998. http://news.bbc.co.uk/2/hi/events/israel_at_50/israel_today/81033.stm.

Sarah McCrum, "Peace Has to Be Between People, You Can't Buy It," *OneWorld.net*, 1993. www.oneworld.org/peacequest/stories/ilkids.html.

Middle East Media Research Institute, "Arafat on the 33rd Anniversary of the Death of Egyptian President Abd Al-Nasser," September 28, 2003. www.memri.de/uebersetzungen_analysen/laender/palaestinensische_a_gebiete/pa_arafat_nasser_02_10_03.pdf.

Judith Miller, "Creating Modern Oman: An Interview with Sultan Qabus," *Foreign Affairs*, May/June 1997. http://www.foreignaffairs.org/19970501facomment3767/judith-miller/creating_modern_oman_an_interview_with_sultanqutos.html.

Bruce Murray, "Making Sense of Fundamentalists," Foundation for American Communications, 2004. www.facsnet.org/issues/faith/antoun.php3.

Ed O'Loughlin, "Running the Snipers' Gauntlet in the West Bank's Frontier of Hate," *Sydney Morning Herald*, June 28, 2003. www.smh.com.au/articles/2003/06/27/1056683906559.html.

PBS, "What Muslims Believe," 2002. www.pbs.org/wgbh/pages/frontline/shows/muslims/etc/what.html.

PBS Frontline, "Who Is Osama Bin Laden?" May 1998. www.jihadunspun.net/BinLadensNetwork/interviews/pbsfrontline05-1998.cfm.

Daniel Pipes, "Greater Syria," Cedarland, 2004. www.geocities.com/CapitolHill/Parliament/2587/syria.html.

Colin L. Powell, "United States Position on Terrorists and Peace in the Middle East," November 19, 2001. Embassy of the Hashimite Kingdom, www.jordanembassyus.org/speech_powell111901.htm.

James J. Puplava, "Riders on the Storm," *Financial Sense Online*, August 16, 2001. www.financialsense.com/series2/riders/shift.htm.

Seyyed Rasuli, "The Pyramid of Skulls: How Saddam Hussein Came to Power," *International Review*, February 20, 2003. www.geocities.com/Paris/Rue/4637/terr37a.html.

Abdulaziz Sachedina, "From Defensive to Offensive Warfare: The Use and Abuse of Jihad in the Muslim World," Organization for Islamic Learning, 2002. www.people.virginia.edu/~aas/article/article8.htm.

Salt Lake Tribune, "Suicide Bombing Elicits Call for Action," October 5, 2003. www.sltrib.com/2003/Oct/10052003/nation_w/98825.asp.

Saudi Arabian Information Source, "Kingdom and Qatar Borders," March 21, 2001. www.saudinf.com/main/y2289.htm.

Howard Schneider, "Iran's Voters Put Pragmatism Above Philosophy," *Washington Post* Foreign Service, February 25, 2000. www.library.cornell.edu/colldev/mideast/irnprag.htm.

Meir Shlomo, "The Arafat Fence," *Providence Journal*, December 9, 2003. www.israelemb.org/boston/fence.html#newman.

Chaim Herzog Center for Middle East Studies and Diplomacy. "The Sinai Agreement," September 4, 1975, www.bgu.ac.il/chcenter/05historical_documents/sinai_agreement.htm.

Maurice Strong, "Peace, Security, and Sustainability," Simon Fraser University, January 16, 2003. www.sfu.ca/blaneyaward/strong_speech2003.htm.

Tim Sullivan, "Women See Few Gains in Kuwait 'Democracy,'" Arab Regional Resource Center on Violence Against Women, December 10, 2002.

www.amanjordan.org/english/daily_news/wmview.php?ArtID=527.

Sydney Morning Herald, "Al-Aqsa Martyrs Brigades Reject Truce," November 20, 2003. www.smh.com.au/articles/2003/11/19/1069027186322.html.

Israel Ministry of Foreign Affairs, "U.N. Security Council Resolution 242," November 22, 1967. www.mfa.gov.il/mfa/go.asp?MFAH00p40.

U.S. Department of State's Office of International Information Programs, "Burns Asks Senate for $200 Million for Middle East Partnership Initiative," March 26, 2003. http://usinfo.state.gov/regional/nea/iraq/text2003/0326burns.htm.

Milton Viorst, "Ayatollah Ruhollah Khomeini," *Time,* April 13, 1998. www.time.com/time/time100/leaders/profile/khomeini.html.

World Zionist Organization, "The Zionist Exposition," 2003. www.wzo.org.il/home/movement/herzl.htm.

Gayle Young, "Rabin's Assassination Has Parallels with Sadat's," CNN, November 6, 1995. www.cnn.com/WORLD/9511/rabin/11-06/index.html.

INDEX

League of Arab States. *See* Arab League

Lebanese Civil War, 45

Lebanon
  Christians and, 23–24
  civil war and, 55
  Greater Syria and, 43, 45
  Hezbollah and, 73
  Litani River and, 38
  peace efforts in, 82–83
  refugees and, 63
  terrorism and, 34
  water conflicts and, 38
  Western control and, 25, 30

Lewis, Bernard, 26

Libya, 10, 26, 46, 77–78

Lockerbie (Scotland), 78

Loeffler, John, 14

Longitudes and Latitudes (Friedman), 78

Lutherans, 23

Macedonia, 12

Mackay, Sandra, 30, 34

MacMahon-Hussein letters of 1915, 28

Mansur Kikhia Foundation for Democracy and Human Rights, 78

Marcus, Jonathan, 20–21

Maronites, 23

Masada, 16

Maxim Restaurant, 66

Mecca, 17

Medina, 17

Mediterranean Sea, 10

Melkites, 23

Middle East
  climate of, 38
  early attempts to control, 10–11
  health care and, 31, 63
  language and, 11
  population of youth in, 73
  trade and, 25
  women and, 20, 49–50, 55

Middle East: A Brief History of the Last 2000 Years, The (Lewis), 26

Middle East Activist, 81–82

Middle East Peace Dialogue Network, 82

Miller, Judith, 51, 55

Mobil, 36

Mohammad Reza Pahlavi, 52, 54–55

monarchy, 49–50

Mosque of the Prophet, 17

Mount of Olives, 18

al-Mubarak, Massoumah, 50

Mubarak, Muhammad Hosni, 49

Muhammad, 17, 22–23

Murphy, Richard, 33

Muslims
  anger toward Americans and, 75
  Christians and, 24
  disputes among, 21–24
  extremists and, 21
  fundamentalists and, 72–73
  government and, 47
  holy wars and, 11
  Jews and, 11, 14
  Kurds and, 30
  Muhammad and, 17
  Ottomans and, 12
  Palestinians and, 14, 19
  sharia and, 72
  Sunni-Shiite conflicts and, 21–24, 30
  Western culture and, 26

Muslim World League, 77

Mustafa Kemal, 25–26, 48–49

Nasser, Gamal Abdel, 43–44, 62

"Nasserist Rule" (article), 44

National Evangelical Church of Beirut, 24

National Geographic Society, 16, 23

nationalism, 30–31, 44

Negev Desert, 38

Nehru, Jawaharlal, 44

"New Water Politics of the Middle East, The" (Berman and Wihbey), 42

Nidhal (Palestinian protester), 65

Nobel Peace Prize, 57–58, 68

Norway, 68, 76, 83

oil
  conflicts over, 12, 40–42
  discovery, effects of, 35
  economy and, 35, 37
  embargo of 1973–1974, 37
  producing nations of, 11–12
  U.S. interests in, 32
  Western control and, 37

Old City, 18

Oman, 10, 12, 42, 49–51

Organization of Arab Petroleum Exporting Countries (OAPEC), 37

Organization of Petroleum Exporting Countries (OPEC), 37

Oslo Peace Accords, 68, 76, 83–84

Ottoman Empire
  ally defeat of, 25
  Greater Syria and, 43
  Islam and, 17
  Middle East invasion by, 12
  republic parliamentary democracy and, 49
  Western culture and, 26
  Western rule and, 30

Pakistan, 77

Palestine
  biblical reference to, 15
  Black September and, 55–56
  Christianity and, 23
  expulsion of non-Jews from, 76
  Greater Syria and, 43

PICTURE CREDITS

Diane Yancey works as a freelance writer in the Pacific Northwest, where she has lived for over twenty years. She writes nonfiction for middle-grade and high school readers and enjoys traveling and collecting old books. Some of her other books include *Life of an American Soldier* (Vietnam War), *Life of an American Soldier* (Korean War), and *Leaders and Generals* (War Against Terrorism).